Jesus is Lord

Jesus is Lord

Christology Yesterday and Today

Donald Macleod

Mentor

ISBN 1 85792 485 1

Published in 2000
by Christian Focus Publications, Geanies House,
Fearn, Ross-shire, IV20 1TW, Great Britain.

Cover design by Owen Daily

Contents

Preface

The various articles which make up this book have at least one thing in common with holy scripture: they were written 'at sundry times and in divers manners'. Some were completed before the invention of *Windows*; others only a few months ago. The first three were omitted (because of lack of space) from my book, *The Person of Christ*, published by Inter-varsity Press in 1998. One ('The Doctrine of the Incarnation in Scottish Theology') is an expanded version of a dictionary article. The other three originally appeared in periodicals.

Despite these variables they are, I hope, uniform in register and style and deal with issues which although of interest to professionals should also engage the minds of all educated Christians. Their common theme is Christ. Their common object is to explore and vindicate his glory.

I am grateful to the publishers, Christian Focus, and particularly their Managing Editor, Malcolm Maclean, for their interest in these articles and for their patience as they missed successive deadlines.

Donald Macleod
Edinburgh
July, 2000.

1

GOD OVER ALL

Many years ago in a famous article in the *Expository Times*, Dr Vincent Taylor asked the question: Does the New Testament call Jesus God?[1] Rudolf Bultmann had given his verdict two decades earlier: 'In describing Christ as *God* the New Testament still exercises great restraint.'[2] Taylor's own conclusion was that there was only one clear ascription of deity to Christ, namely, the words of Thomas in John 20:28, 'My Lord and my God.' In a later article in the *Expository Times*, Dr Michael Austin dismissed even John 20:28 on the ground that it was contradicted by the earlier words of John 20:17 ('I ascend to my Father and your Father, to my God and your God') and concluded: 'The New Testament makes no unambiguous claim to Jesus' divinity, if by this is meant identity of nature with God the Father.'[3]

All this will come as a considerable surprise to ordinary readers of the New Testament. The Revised Standard Version ascribes the designation *God* to Jesus in four passages: John 1:1, John 20:28, Titus 2:13 and 2 Peter 1:1. The New International Version adds three more: John 1:18, Romans 9:5 and Hebrews 1:8. But all these renderings have been challenged and therefore require careful examination.

The difficulty with John 1:1 is that John omits the definite article before God: *theos ēn ho logos*. This has led to suggestions (for example, by Jehovah's Witnesses) that the statement should be translated 'the Word was *a* god'. Apart from every other consideration, this would be a revolutionary announcement to come from the pen of a Jewish monotheist. More credibly, James Moffat offered the rendering, 'the Logos was divine', arguing from the absence of the article that *theos* was an adjective. This rendering has the effect of blurring the distinction between Christ and men in general, since the latter, too, can be said to be partakers of the divine nature. Yet it has commanded considerable support.

9

Don Cupitt, for example, follows Moffat's approach.[4] Vincent Taylor, too, in the article already cited, regards the omission of the article as decisive. He even conveys the impression that Moffat's translation is now the generally accepted one and that very few scholars regard the passage as teaching that Christ is God in the absolute sense of the name.

There is no grammatical reason, however, to depart from the traditional rendering. Had John wanted to say *divine* the adjective *theios* was ready to hand. In the sentence which he did actually write, the omission of the article is a matter of word order. *Theos* is a predicate noun and it is a generally accepted rule that 'when a predicate noun precedes a verb it lacks the definite article: grammatical considerations therefore require that there be no doctrinal significance in the dropping of the article, for it is simply a matter of word order.'[5] Furthermore, it is clear from the context and from the whole of the ensuing Gospel that John would have had few reservations about calling Jesus *God*. He describes him as one who was in the beginning, never coming into being, but being eternally. He affirms that all things were made by him (verse 3) and that what existed lived in him (verse 4). In fact, even some who reject the translation *God* go on to interpret the passage in such exalted terms that one wonders what their reservations are. G.H.C. MacGregor, for example, declares, 'John does not say "The Logos was God",' and yet goes on to interpret the residual statement as meaning, 'The Logos was partaker of the divine essence.'[6] If John believed that, why should we appeal to 'unfounded grammatical principle' to deny that he could call his Saviour *God*?

It is unlikely, however, that the particular form of John's statement is due to grammatical considerations alone. John could have chosen a different word order, putting the predicate *after* the noun. This would have allowed him to write *ho theos*. In all probability, however, he had a theological aversion to applying this designation to the Word. *Ho theos* was the Father. The Word was with *ho theos,* but he was not himself *ho theos*. He was not the One he was with. Alternatively, the addition of the article would have meant that the Word was the godhead: no divine being existed except the Word. As B.F. Westcott pointed out, however, this is pure Sabellianism: The Father and the Spirit are also *theos*.[7]

John 1:18 presents a different problem. The AV, RV, RSV and NIV all read, 'the only begotten Son'. The margins of both the RV and the NIV, however, suggest the reading *God* as an alternative to *Son*. This is in fact the reading adopted by the United Bible Societies' Greek New Testament (3rd Edition): *monogenēs theos*. It is certainly well attested (Aleph, B, C, 33, Boh, Pesh, Gnostics, Irenaeus, Clement, Origen, Gregory of Nyssa and others) and this attestation has been strengthened by the recent discovery of the two papyrus fragments, *p66* and *p45*, both of which read *monogenēs theos*.

There is another consideration, too: *monogenēs theos* is undoubtedly the more difficult reading. *ho monogenēs huios* can be accounted for by assimilation to such passages as John 3:16 ('his only begotten Son'). By contrast, the phrase *monogenēs theos* occurs only here in the New Testament. There is also the problem of the definite article. If the original reading had been *ho monogenēs huios* it is difficult to see how the article could have dropped out: a scribe would simply have read *theos* for *huios* (or even *ths* for *hs*) but the article would have remained. If, however, John had originally written *theos* he is likely to have kept it anarthrous as in John 1:1.

According to Sir Edward Hoskyns,[8] 'The immediate context seems to be decisive; for "who is in the bosom of the Father" almost requires "only begotten Son".' Barrett shares this view: '*huios* seems to be imperatively demanded by the following clause, and is in conformity with Johannine usage.'[9] It may equally well be argued, however, that these were the very considerations that led scribes to alter an original reading *theos* for *huios*. It is very difficult to understand how the reverse process (altering *huios* to *theos*) could have taken place.

John 20:28 is free of any obvious difficulty: 'Thomas answered him, 'My Lord and my God!" (*ho kurios mou kai ho theos mou*). Dr Michael Austin, as we have seen, argues that these words are contradicted by John 20:17. Even if this were true, John 20:28 still calls Jesus *God*. But it is difficult to take Dr Austin's argument

seriously. The idea of Christ ascending 'to my Father and your
Father, to my God and your God' is quite compatible with his
deity. Indeed, one very clear implication of these words, as has
been pointed out times without number, is that Jesus' relation to
the Father was quite different from the disciples'. He does not
say, '*Our* Father' or '*Our* God' but, '*my* Father and *your* Father,
my God and *your* God.' The relationships are not symmetrical.
God is his Father in a unique sense and God is his God in a unique
sense. That sense did not, however, preclude reverence. By the
incarnation Christ had come into a position of servitude and
dependence. He had to finish the work given to him. He had to be
upheld by the Father's Spirit (Isa. 42:1). No one has expressed these
ideas more unambiguously than John: 'the Father is greater than
I' (John 14:28). Christian theology has easily accommodated this
kind of subordination by speaking of it as economical rather than
ontological. It is an inevitable result (and maybe even the very
essence) of the incarnation. By becoming a servant, the One who
was equal with God put himself in a position where God was his
God. There is nothing in that incompatible with the claim that
Christ is *theos*. John clearly intended the words, 'My Lord and
my God!' to form the climax of his Gospel: there is virtual
unanimity that Chapter 21 is a later addition. John's whole message
is set between the affirmation, 'The Word was God' and the
confession, 'My Lord and my God!'. These provide the framework
for all he has to say. If they are not true, then the claims John
makes for Jesus are blasphemous.

The Epistle to the Hebrews
In the Epistle to the Hebrews the only passage where the writer
appears to call Jesus *God* is 1:8: 'But of the Son he says, "Your
throne, O God, will last for ever and ever".' Even so conservative
a scholar as B.F. Westcott, however, dismissed this rendering of
the original, preferring, 'God is thy throne' (the reading of the
RSV Margin). 'It is scarcely possible,' wrote Westcott, 'that
Elohim in the original can be addressed to the King. The
presumption therefore is against the belief that *ho theos* is a
vocative in the LXX.'[10]

To say the least, however, the proposition *God is your throne* (or, *Your throne is God*) would be highly unusual. Turner even goes so far as to call it 'grotesque'.[11] The rendering, 'Your throne, O God', suits the context well. The Son's superiority to the angels is seen in that while *they* serve the throne, *he* sits on it: and he does so precisely because he is *Son*. It is noteworthy, too, that in the following quotation (from Psalm 102:25-27) the Son is addressed as *Lord*, using an undoubted vocative, *kurie*. Nor is there really much substance in the claim that the King could not be addressed as *Elohim*. In Psalm 82:6 the rulers of Israel are called precisely that: 'I said, You are *"gods"*; you are all sons of the Most High.' As F.F. Bruce points out, 'To Hebrew poets and prophets a prince of the house of David was the vicegerent of Israel's God... what was only partially true of any of the historical rulers of David's line, or even of David himself, would be realised in its fulness when that Son of David appeared in whom all the promises and ideals associated with that dynasty would be embodied... this Messiah can be addressed not only as God's Son but actually as God, for he is both the Messiah of David's line and also the effulgence of God's glory and the very image of his substance.'[12] Bruce's observations are borne out by the fact that in the Old Testament the Messiah is addressed both as 'Mighty God' (Isa. 9:6) and as 'Jehovah our Righteousness' (Jer. 23:6). Psalm 45 is not therefore unique in calling him *elohim*.

Does Paul Call Jesus God?

According to Frances Young, Paul nowhere calls Jesus *God*.[13] The same sentiment is expressed by C.H. Dodd: 'Even though he ascribes to Christ functions and dignities which are consistent with nothing less than deity, yet he pointedly avoids calling him "God".'[14] In fact this view was already being advocated by Charles Anderson Scott in 1927. Scott not only stated categorically that 'St. Paul did not call Jesus Christ God', but went on to pronounce that any uncertainty as to this question (in the light of such passages as Romans 9:5) 'must give way before the very great improbability that one in whom the monotheistic faith of Judaism was so deeply ingrained could have taken this momentous step'.[15]

Despite these confident claims, however, there are several passages where, *prima facie,* Paul certainly appears to call Jesus *God*.

The earliest of these is 2 Thessalonians 1:12, the one passage
where, according to Bultmann, it seems probable that Paul
describes Christ as God.[16] In the King James Version the rendering
is: 'That the name of our Lord Jesus Christ may be glorified in
you, and ye in him, according to the grace of our God and the
Lord Jesus Christ.' It can be argued, however, that the concluding
phrase should read, 'according to the grace of our God and Lord
Jesus Christ.' The basis of the argument is that since there is only
one definite article covering both names, God and Lord, the
reference must be to one person, 'our God and Lord'. This is
certainly grammatically possible, but it is by no means certain in
view of the fact that 'Lord' is a proper name and can thus be
definite even without the article. Furthermore, it is Paul's habitual
practice, as exemplified even by this epistle itself, to ascribe grace
to a two-fold source. For example, both in 1 Thessalonians 1:1
and 2 Thessalonians 1:2 he writes, 'Grace to you and peace, from
God our Father and the Lord Jesus Christ.' It is difficult in the
light of these considerations to affirm with any certainty that in 2
Thessalonians 1:12 the designation 'our God' refers to 'the Lord
Jesus Christ'.

We seem to be on more solid ground in Acts 20:28, which in
the New International Version reads, 'Be shepherds of the church
of God, which he bought with his own blood.' According to this
rendering, the person who shed his blood for the redemption of
the Church is clearly identified as *God*. There are, however, certain
difficulties facing this interpretation.

In the first place, there is some uncertainty as to the phrase,
'the church of God'. Many manuscripts have the alternative reading
'the church of the Lord' and on textual evidence alone it is difficult
to be certain as to what exactly the Apostle said. The best uncial
manuscripts favour *God*, the best minuscules favour *Lord* and the
most witnesses favour the conflated reading *Lord and God* (in
various combinations). Most modern editors, however, favour the
reading 'the church of God' and there are cogent reasons for this.
The manuscripts which favour it – including Codex Vaticanus

and Codex Sinaiticus – are of excellent authority. Furthermore, the passage is an evident allusion to Psalm 74:2: 'Remember thy congregation, which thou hast purchased of old' (RV). The church (congregation) is here clearly conceived of as the 'church of God'. This reading is also supported by internal considerations. Paul's whole concern is to impress the elders with a due sense of their responsibility by emphasising the dignity of the church, and nothing could do this more effectively than to portray it as 'the church of God'. Finally, *theou* (God) is obviously the more difficult reading. It is hard to understand why anybody should wish to change *Lord* to *God*, but perfectly comprehensible that some should wish to soften the paradox of 'the blood of God' by substituting *Lord*. This motive would operate among different sections of the early church; among the Arians who denied the deity of Christ; among those who detested the doctrine of the Patripassians that it was the Father who suffered; and among simple, orthodox believers, offended by the sharp contrast implied in *the blood of God*. On the other hand, there was nothing offensive to anyone in the reading *Lord*.

The other difficulty in this passage relates to the phrase 'his own blood'. Some suggest that this is a mis-translation and that the correct rendering is 'the blood of his own'. This is apparently supported by the fact that in the papyri the phrase 'his own' was often used as a term of endearment, equivalent to 'his beloved' or to Paul's phrase in Colossians 1:13, 'the Son of his love'. The traditional translation, however, is equally tenable grammatically and is only suspect because it implies the idea of the *blood of God*, to which so many scholars, ancient and modern, are averse. It does not seem to have occurred to the Fathers, however, that this offensive paradox could be avoided by adopting the translation 'the blood of his own'. The variations in the manuscripts suggest that the only solution which suggested itself to them was to substitute *Lord* for *God*.

The third Pauline passage to be considered is Romans 9:5. Here again, according to the New International Version, Paul specifically calls Christ *God*: 'Theirs are the patriarchs, and from them is traced the human ancestry of Christ, who is God over all, for ever praised.' This interpretation follows the Authorised Version and the Revised Version. Some other versions, however, (including Moffat, the Revised Standard Version and the Good News Bible) punctuate the passage differently. They insert a full stop after *flesh* and construe the remaining words of the verse as an independent doxology to God the Father: 'May God who is over all be blessed for ever!' This effectively eliminates the ascription of the designation *God* to Christ.

The problem, as Sanday and Headlam point out,[17] is one of interpretation and not of criticism, since the original manuscripts contained no punctuation. The balance of evidence strongly favours the rendering adopted by the New International Version.

First, the vast majority of the Christian writers of the first eight centuries refer the words to Christ. These include Irenaeus, Hippolytus, Cyprian, Athanasius, Gregory of Nyssa, Chrysostom, Augustine, Hilary and Ambrose. Only two writers, Photius and Dioderus, are definitely known to ascribe the words to the Father.

Two quotations will suffice, the first from Athanasius: 'If indeed our Saviour is neither God, nor the Word, nor the Son,' he writes, 'then let the Arians be no longer ashamed to think and talk as pagans and Jews do. But if he is the Word, and the proper Son of his Father; if he is God of God and "over all, blessed for ever", then shall we not utterly destroy this "Thalia", this novel doctrine and language of Arius as if it were some horrible idol?'[18]

Augustine writes to the same effect: 'He may be rightly understood to be the Saviour himself, of whom the Apostle says, "Whose are the fathers, and of whom as concerning the flesh Christ came, who is over all, God blessed for ever".'[19] There is no reason to think that this virtually unanimous interpretation on the part of the Fathers was dictated by any controversial interest. It was characteristic not only of the orthodox but also of the Gnostics and Arians, who did not regard Christ as divine. On the other hand, the orthodox had a certain interest in avoiding it because it might seem to favour the Sabellian view that the Son and the Father were one Person. In any case, the interpretation adopted by the New International Version clearly rests on a very ancient tradition carrying us back virtually to the times of the Apostles themselves.

Secondly, the words 'according to the flesh' naturally lead us to expect an antithesis, and such an antithesis is provided by the phrase 'God over all'. The situation here is very similar to that in Romans 1:3-4 where the phrase 'according to the flesh' (*kata sarka*) is balanced by its antithesis, 'according to the Spirit'. Paul has been led in the course of his argument to emphasise our Lord's humanness and Jewishness, and this one-sidedness requires to be corrected by introducing the other aspect, the cosmic sovereignty and deity of the Saviour. Of course, this is only an expectation and it is not absolutely inevitable that it should be met. But the natural impression on the mind of the reader would be that the contrast with *kata sarka* which he has been led to expect is provided by the words which follow.

Thirdly, the natural interpretation of the words *ho ōn* (literally, 'who being') is to take them as equivalent to *hos esti* ('who is'). As such, they would have to refer back to their antecedent, like any other relative pronoun; and the only possible antecedent is *Christ*. In the few instances where *ho ōn* does not refer backwards (as in John 3:31) the form of the sentence is such as to make plain that there is a change of subject, and thus to place the meaning beyond doubt. In Romans 9:5, there is a noun immediately preceding, to which *ho ōn* might naturally refer. Furthermore, if a new subject (God) is introduced there is no finite verb in the closing part of the verse to describe the action performed by this subject. The mind is led to infer from the whole tendency of the sentence that the words 'who is above all' refer backwards to Christ.

The same conclusion follows from the position of *eulogētos* (blessed). If the concluding part of Romans 9:5 were an ascription of blessing to God the Father we would expect *eu logētos* to stand first, exactly as the word *blessed* would in a doxology in English. This is the normal form of doxology in both the Septuagint and the rest of the New Testament. For example, in 2 Corinthians 1:3, the order is 'Blessed be God, even the Father of our Lord Jesus Christ.' The same is true of Ephesians 1:3, 'Blessed be the God and Father of our Lord Jesus Christ.' This rule is not absolutely invariable. There may sometimes be a need to give emphasis to a particular word in a doxology and then that word, rather than *blessed*, is placed first. But the burden of proof lies on those who maintain that in this passage Paul is departing from normal usage.

So far as grammar is concerned, then, if the reference of the words 'who is over all' is to Christ, everything is natural and as we might expect. If, on the other hand, the words refer to God the Father, everything is unusual: the absence of an antithesis to *according to the flesh*, the forward reference of *ho ōn* and the position of the word *eulogētos*.

Two further considerations also favour the interpretation adopted by the New International Version.

First, it fits the context admirably. In this case, as Cullmann points out, 'the enumeration of the signs of Israel's election reaches a climax in the statement that from Israel comes one according to the flesh who is simply "over all".'[20] On the other hand, the sudden introduction of a doxology is inconsistent with the tone of sadness which pervades the passage. It is true that it was a fairly common practice among the Rabbis to add a doxology whenever the name of God was used. But this hardly fits the circumstances in this particular case. The name of God has not been used and is introduced (on this theory) only for the sake of the doxology itself.

Secondly, the translation adopted in the NIV accords with Pauline usage elsewhere. C.H. Dodd rejects this way of construing the words on the ground that 'such a direct application of the term "God" to Christ would be unique in Paul's writings'.[21] But this is surely to beg the question. Dodd himself concedes that Paul ascribes to Christ functions and prerogatives consistent with nothing less than deity and there can be no doubt that Paul's view of the glory of Christ was such that it was perfectly natural for him to designate him *God* even if only occasionally. Only in explicitness does the designation *God* here stand out as unusual.

Nor is there anything unlikely in Paul's ascribing a doxology to Christ. Other New Testament writers do it. There is such a doxology, for example, in 2 Peter 3:18, 'But grow in the grace and knowledge of our Lord and Saviour Jesus Christ. To him be glory both now and for ever! Amen.' We find another instance of the same thing in Revelation 5:13, 'Then I heard every creature in heaven... singing, "To him who sits on the throne and to the Lamb/ be praise and honour and glory and power/ for ever and ever."'

It is, then, virtually certain that in Romans 9:5 Paul calls Jesus *God*. The same is true of Titus 2:13 which reads, in the Authorised Version, 'Looking for that blessed hope, and the glorious appearing of the great God and our Saviour Jesus Christ.' Many other versions, however (including the NIV, the Revised Version, the Revised Standard Version and the Good News Bible), take the passage as referring to an appearing of only one person: 'Looking for that blessed hope and the appearing of the glory of our great God and Saviour, Jesus Christ.' This interpretation is favoured by the grammar and virtually demanded by the context. The fact that there is a single definite article covering the two names, *God* and *Saviour*, strongly suggests that only one person is in view. Furthermore, the adjective *great* is rather pointless as applied to God the Father but highly significant if applied to Christ: not only because it highlights the expected glory of his *parousia* but also because it serves to place in sharp relief the humiliation and condescension implied in the words which follow, (the great God) 'who gave himself for us'. Again, Christians are not expecting any appearing or second coming of God the Father. In the Pauline writings, the appearing (*epiphany*) of the glory is always associated with Jesus Christ. We see this, for example, in 2 Thessalonians 2:8, where he writes: 'whom the Lord Jesus will destroy with the breath of his mouth and destroy by the splendour (*epiphany*) of his coming.' The blessed hope, surely, is that the Lord, not God the Father, will descend from heaven.

When we add that it was not God the Father who gave himself for us but specifically Jesus Christ, the argument is surely conclusive in favour of the view that in Titus 2:13 Jesus is designated *God*.[22]

Second Peter 1:1

There remains the statement of 2 Peter 1:1, which the Revised Standard Version translates, 'Simon Peter, a servant and apostle of Jesus Christ, to those who have obtained a faith of equal standing with ours in the righteousness of our God and Saviour Jesus Christ.'

The difficulty here is exactly the same as in Titus 2:13: Does the phrase *tou theou hēmōn kai sōtēros* refer to one person or to two? Is it 'the righteousness of God and of our Saviour' or 'the righteousness of our God and Saviour'? The grammar strongly favours the latter. The rule that 'where two substantives refer to the one person, it is usual to omit the article' is indeed not invariable. There are exceptions. But then, they *are* exceptions and as Turner points out,[23] 'If there be ambiguity, correct grammatical principles ought to be decisive.'

In fact, there are clear instances of the same construction in this very epistle and in every one of them scholars adhere unhesitatingly to the single reference. The nearest example is in 2 Peter 1:11: 'you will receive a rich welcome into the eternal kingdom of *our Lord and Saviour Jesus Christ.*' No one doubts that in this instance both *Lord* and *Saviour* refer to the one person, Jesus Christ. Where, on the other hand, the writer wishes to make a distinction (to refer to two different persons) his construction is different. We have an example as close as 2 Peter 1:2: 'Grace and peace be yours in abundance through the knowledge of God and of Jesus our Lord' (*en epignōsē tou theou kai Iēsou tou kuriou hēmōn*).

But it is not a matter of grammar alone. If we take Peter's statement as referring to two subjects, *our* can refer only to *God* and *Saviour Jesus Christ* is left standing awkwardly on its own: 'in the righteousness of our God and of Saviour Jesus Christ.' Furthermore, where *Saviour* occurs elsewhere in this epistle, it is always in a combination similar to 'our God and Saviour'. For example, in 1:11, 2:20, 3:2 and 3:18 we have the combination 'our Lord and Saviour'. Nor would there be anything at all surprising about Peter's calling Jesus *God*. Not only do John, Paul and the writer to the Hebrews do the same (if our argument so far has been correct), but Peter closes this epistle with a doxology to Jesus: 'Grow in the grace and knowledge of our Lord and Saviour Jesus Christ. To him be the glory both now and to the day of eternity.' Such a doxology presupposes the highest possible view of the grandeur of Jesus. In fact, there is good evidence that Peter and the other leaders of the early Christian community deliberately applied to their Saviour the most grandiose titles which pagan rulers arrogated to themselves. The designation, 'Our great God and Saviour' was one of these. It appears frequently in papyrus fragments of the Ptolemaic and Imperial periods.[24]

The Apostolic Fathers

H.W. Montefiore makes an interesting comment on Hebrews 1:8: 'The author must have been accustomed to the outright ascription of divinity to the Son, for he shows not the slightest embarrassment.'[25] That it did indeed become customary and natural is clear from the Apostolic Fathers. The title occurs repeatedly, for example, in the Epistles of Ignatius, written in the early years of the second century. In his Epistle to the Romans he writes, 'Our God, Jesus the Christ, was conceived in the womb by Mary' (18). He uses the title again in the Epistle to the Smyrneans, 'I give glory to Jesus Christ the God' (1); and in his Epistle to Polycarp, 'I bid you farewell always in our God Jesus Christ' (8). We find the same usage in the so-called Second Epistle of Clement to the Romans: 'Brethren, we ought so to think of Jesus Christ as of God' (1).

Yet even in these later writers the designation *God* is used with remarkable economy. Why such reserve in both the apostolic and sub-apostolic literature? There are at least three reasons.

First, early Christian theology was wrought out in the context of worship and devotion. They prayed to him, called on him and sang doxologies to him. The natural idiom for this was *kurie* (Lord), a vocative, not *theos* (God).

Secondly, there was the usage of Christ himself. It would have been unnatural for him to refer to himself as God. He thought of himself, relationally, as the Son and addressed God as *Abba* (Father). This was fully reflected, with respect to both Persons, in the later discourse of the church.

Thirdly, the very nature of salvation meant that the emphasis must fall on the title Son of God rather than on God absolutely. The consummation of the work of redemption highlighted for the first time the distinctions within the godhead. It would have been confusing to refer constantly to both the Father and the Son as *theos*. The terminology had to reflect the relationship between them: and that was best done, in the Saviour's case, by calling him *Son, Word* or *Servant*. Moreover, at key points (for example, John 3:16, Romans 8:32) the New Testament shows a clear desire to focus on the activity of God the Father, almost as if it were deliberately seeing the cross in the light of the story of Abraham offering up Isaac. In these passages the stress falls on the Father's initiative and love. *He* did not spare. *he* gave. *He* delivered up. Such a framework required an emphasis on the distinctions, as well as on the fact that Christ was both *monogenēs* and *agapētos*. Thus, while it was natural to invoke Christ as Lord it was natural to reflect on him as Son.

The Christ-hymn of Philippians
In Philippians 2:6 Paul refers to Christ in a way which falls little short of calling him *God*. He speaks of him as being 'in the form of God' (*en morphē theou*). The passage is important not only in its own right, but because it is the key to one of the richest veins of New Testament Christology. In a well known study, J.B. Lightfoot concluded that *morphē* was the specific character or essence of a thing.[26] He based this conclusion on the use of the word in Plato, Aristotle and later philosophers such as Plutarch. In these writers, a firm distinction is drawn between *morphē* and *schēma*. *Schēma* is the changing, fleeting shape or appearance. *Morphē* is permanent. It is the abstract conception realised, the impress of the idea on the individual essence or object. B.B. Warfield[27] agreed with Lightfoot: 'Form,' he wrote, 'is a term which expresses the sum of those characterising qualities which make a thing the precise thing that it is. ... When our Lord is said to be "in the form of God," therefore, he is declared in the most express manner possible, to be all that God is, to possess the whole fulness of the attributes which make God God.'

It is highly debatable, however, whether the usage of classical philosophy can be accepted as decisive for the New Testament. It belongs to a different period and a different culture. It is certainly very difficult, with regard to the New Testament, to maintain the *morphē/schēma* distinction consistently. In Mark 16:12, for example, we are told that Christ appeared to his disciples in *another form*. Here *morphē* is clearly synonymous with *schēma*. The Lord's *appearance* had changed. Even some of the instances quoted by Lightfoot in support of his own case really point in the opposite direction: 'We are transformed (*metamorphoumetha*) into the same image' (2 Cor. 3:18); 'Be transformed (*metamorphousthe*) by the renewing of your mind' (Rom. 12:2). Surely the very point here is that *morphē* is not permanent. It may be changed (while the essence still remains). The same is true of Jesus' Transfiguration (Matt. 17:2; Mark 9:2). His *morphē* was changed but his essence was not. To adapt Warfield's words, he did not cease to possess the sum total of those characteristics which made him exactly who and what he was.

The clue to the meaning of *morphē* is probably to be found not in the classical philosophers but in the Septuagint. This is the approach taken by, among others, R.P. Martin.[28] In the Septuagint *morphē* is virtually synonymous with *eidos* and *homoioma*, the usual words for *appearance*. This can be seen from such passages as Job 4:16, Isaiah 44:13 and Daniel 3:19. Job 4:16, for example, reads: 'It (a spirit) stood still, but I could not discern its *appearance*. A *form* was before my eyes; there was silence, then I heard a voice' (RSV). The parallelism here makes clear that appearance and form (*homoioma* and *morphē*) are synonymous. *Morphē* is the appearance appropriate to God.

But how can this be, since God is invisible? What appearance or form can be appropriate to God? The answer can only be: 'his glory!' This is what, according to John, Isaiah saw (John 12:41; Isaiah 6:1). It is also what Christ had with the Father before the world was (John 17:5). When Paul speaks of Christ as being in the form of God he is claiming that Christ was no other than the glory (*doxa*) of God.

But this is not a matter of mere inference. It is supported by several direct lines of evidence. For one thing, *morphē* is closely related not only to *eidos* and *homoioma*, but also to *eikon* and *doxa*. In the Septuagint, *eikon*, *morphē* and *doxa* are used interchangeably to render the two Hebrew words *tselem* and *demuth*. For example, in Daniel 3:19, *tselem* is rendered by

morphē; in Genesis 1:26, it is rendered by *eikon*. The synonymous
Hebrew word *demuth* is usually rendered by *eikon*; but in Numbers
12:8 it is rendered by *doxa* and in Job 4:16 it is rendered by
morphē. It is fair to conclude that the three words *eikon, morphē*
and *doxa* are broadly synonymous; and that they were closely
associated with the Hebrew words *tselem* and *demuth*.

The effects of this can be clearly seen in the New Testament in
the various allusions to Genesis 1:27, 'So God created man in his
own image.' In 1 Corinthians 11:7, for example, Paul alludes to
the passage in the words, 'man is the image and glory (*eikon kai
doxa*) of God.' In 2 Corinthians 4:4, he speaks of 'the light of the
gospel of the glory of Christ, who is the *image* (*eikon*) of God'.
Yet two verses later he speaks of 'the knowledge of the *glory*
(*doxa*) of God in the face of Jesus Christ.'

We are left, then, with three closely related concepts.

First, Christ is the *image* of God. The most emphatic statement
of this is in Colossians 1:15: 'Christ who is the image of the invisible God.' In the immediate context, Paul is emphasising the cosmic functions of Christ: he antedates creation; creation was made
through him; he holds it together; it exists for him; all other exist-
ences (especially angelic principalities and powers) are totally
dependent on him. But all this rests on something deeper: he is
the image of God. His functional superiority rests on ontological
pre-eminence. He has a unique relation to God. He is his image;
and this image must have sufficient content to bear the weight of
the context. Furthermore, all the fullness (*pan to plērōma*) dwells
in him (Col. 1:19). The same term occurs in Colossians 2:9 where
its meaning is more explicit: all the fullness *of the godhead* (*tēs
theotētos*) dwells in him. According to Lightfoot, *plērōma* is 'a
recognised technical term in theology, denoting the totality of the
Divine powers and attributes.'[29] It is reminiscent of the form *elohim* in the Old Testament, the plural (of intensity) suggesting that
the whole of *el*-ness, which polytheism distributed over a vast
number of deities, is in the religion of revelation concentrated in
one God who possesses in himself all divine energies. Christ owes
his position as the one Mediator and the sole Lord of creation to
the fact that as the image of God he possesses all the *plērōma*:

the concentrated fullness of divine qualities, powers and prerogatives.

We must not forget, however, that Paul refers to him specifically as the image of the invisible (*aoratos*) God. It is in Christ that the God who is hidden becomes visible. The image is a true representation of the divine being at the most profound level: a point made even more emphatically by Hebrews 1:3, which speaks of Christ as the *express image* (*charaktēr*) of God's substance (*hupostasis*).

This brings us to the second concept: Christ is the *glory* of God. This has obvious Old Testament roots, one of the most interesting passages being Ezekiel 1:26-28, where the prophet's vision of God culminates in the statement, 'Such was the appearance of the likeness of the glory of the LORD,' and there follows, 'And when I saw it, I fell upon my face, and I heard the voice of one speaking.' It seems clear from this that the glory was not merely a detached manifestation. God was *in* the manifestation. The Glory itself spoke. The Glory itself was to be worshipped.

In the New Testament, the most interesting passage is James 2:1. Many versions, including the Authorised Version and the Revised Standard Version render the passage as follows: 'My brethren, have no partiality as you hold the faith of our Lord Jesus Christ, the Lord of glory.' But this involves arbitrarily inserting a second *Lord* before *glory*. Bengel favoured a literal translation, where Christ himself is called the Glory: 'Show no partiality as you hold the faith of our Lord Jesus Christ, the Glory.' Such commentators as Mayor and Hort agreed.

Bengel's interpretation is well justified. There is an exactly similar construction in 1 Timothy 1:1 which the versions unanimously render, 'Paul an apostle of Christ Jesus by command of God our Saviour and of Christ Jesus *our hope*.' If we can speak of Jesus our hope, why not of Jesus the glory? As Hort points out,[30] it suits the context perfectly: 'The faith of Christ as the Glory was peculiarly at variance with the favouritism shown to the rich: since he who represented the very majesty of heaven was distinguished by his lowliness and poverty. As St. James rebukes the cursing of men who are made in the image of God, so here he rebukes the contemptuous usage of poor men, such as the Incarnate Glory of Christ himself became.'

Furthermore, other similar expressions are applied to Christ elsewhere in the New Testament. He is called the Truth, the Life and, above all, the Word. Again, Hort's comment is apposite: 'Now the Word of the Targums is the true antecedent of the Logos of St. John, much more so than the Logos of Philo; and it would be only natural that the other great conception which linked God to men, that of the Glory, should be transferred to Christ as the true Fulfiller of it.'

Bengel's interpretation is also supported by the fact that elsewhere in the New Testament the word *doxa* is clearly used of a Person. This may be true, for example, in Ephesians 1:17, 'the God of our Lord Jesus Christ, the Father of the Glory.' It is certainly the case in 1 Peter 4:14, 'If you are reproached for the name of Christ, you are blessed, because the Spirit of the Glory and of God rests upon you.' In 2 Peter 1:17, the expression 'the excellent glory' (*megaloprepous doxēs*) is a periphrasis for God himself. Parallel expressions are also applied to God. Hebrews 1:3 tells us that Christ sat down at the right hand of the Majesty (*tēs megalōsunēs*); and in Matthew 26:64 the Lord himself tells his judges that one day they will see him sitting at the right hand of the Power (*tēs dunameōs*).

It is interesting, too, that in both the Old Testament and Jewish expectation the glory (*kabhodh*) was interpreted messianically and eschatologically. The words of Psalm 85:9, for example, were applied to the Messiah: 'that glory (the Shekinah) may dwell in our land.' The prophet Zechariah records the Lord as promising, with respect to the last days: 'I, saith the LORD, will be the Glory in the midst' (Zech. 2:5). And in *Pirque Aboth* there is an interesting commentary on the well-known word of Matthew 18:20 ('Whenever two or three gather together in my name, there am I in the midst'): 'Two that sit together and are occupied in words of Torah have the Shekinah among them.'

There seems little reason, then, to doubt that the correct rendering of James 2:1 is, 'The Lord Jesus Christ, the glory.' James, although brought up as a member of the same family as Jesus (surely the most likely way to be disillusioned), did not scruple to apply to him the sacred name, Lord. Few scruples could have remained about calling him *the Glory*. It is significant, too, as Mayor points out, that the word *doxa* stands alone without *hēmōn* (our) or *tou patros* (of the Father): 'It is in order that it may be understood in its fullest sense of him who alone comprises all glory in himself.'[31] Christ is God seen and revealed. In him the God of the Bush and the God of Sinai and the God who dwelt between the Cherubim continues to be present with his people. This is both an encouragement (Matt. 28:20) and a deterrent. The story of Ananias and Sapphira (Acts 5:1-11) illustrates the trauma created for the believing community by the fact that God dwelt among them: 'Be ye holy, because I am holy' (1 Pet. 1:16).

There are clear allusions to the *Shekinah* in at least two other New Testament passages. One is Revelation 21:3, 'The tabernacle (*skēnē*) of God is with men': compare Leviticus 26:11, 'I will place my *skēnē* in the midst of you.' The other is John 1:14, 'The Word became flesh, and dwelt (*eskēnōsen*) among us (and we saw his glory...full of grace and truth).'

Anthony Tyrrell Hanson has examined this latter passage thoroughly in *Grace and Truth: A Study in the Doctrine of the Incarnation*.[32] The most important fact, according to Hanson, is that the words *grace and truth* (*charis kai alētheia*) are taken from Exodus 34:6-7: 'The LORD passed before him and proclaimed, "The LORD, the LORD, a God merciful and gracious, slow to anger and abounding in *steadfast love* and faithfulness (*hesed we 'emeth*)." ' The occasion was a momentous one. Moses had asked to see God's glory and this was God's response. Grace and truth were covenant concepts, emphasising God's undeviating commitment to his people. That the Old Testament background was present to John's mind is clear from verse 17: 'For the law came through Moses, but grace and truth came through Jesus Christ.' By alluding to the incident on Sinai and using covenant language John is reminding the reader that the God who revealed himself to Moses has now revealed himself (and his new covenant) in Jesus Christ. *Glory*, as we have seen, is synonymous with *image*. It is concerned with God manifested. God is invisible, but he has become visible in Jesus: 'No man has ever seen God. The only-begotten Son, being in the bosom of the Father, *he* has explained him' (verse 18). The Glory is the Exegesis of God. But the Exegesis is possible only because he and the Father are one being (*hen esmen*, John 10:30), so that anyone who has seen Christ has seen the Father (John 14:9). Even more interesting, however, is the relation between the glory on the one hand and grace and truth on the other. Historically, Christian thought has seen these as belonging to opposite ends of the spectrum of divine holiness. Glory belonged to the *mysterium tremendum*: grace and truth (faithfulness) to the *mysterium fascinans*. Glory repels. Grace and faithfulness attracts. John (or, rather, the revelation he describes) breaks through all that. Not only is there no tension between glory and grace. The glory *is* the grace. Not that this was by any means a New Testament discovery. It was already implicit in Exodus 34:6-7. It was clear, too, in Micah 7:18: 'Who is a God like thee, that pardons iniquity and passes by the transgression of the remnant of his heritage? He does not retain his anger for ever, because he delights in mercy.' But it is in the New Testament that this is revealed with dramatic force and clarity. The glory of God as defined in Jesus Christ is that he is One who enters into covenant with sinners and commits himself to them in terms of the most steadfast love and loyalty. The 'riches of his glory' (Eph. 3:16) are precisely the same as 'the riches of his grace' (Eph. 1:7).

Christ, The Form of God

When we turn to the third concept, *morphē*, the ideas associated with *eikon* and *doxa* (as well as with *plēroma* and *charakter*) are already firmly fixed in our minds. In the context of Philippians 2:5-11, the *morphē theou* refers to a pre-existent state. Unlike the rest of us, the Lord's human, earthly existence is a matter of deliberate choice. He made a decision not to cling to equality with God but to make himself nothing. He could not, when already a servant, have chosen to become a servant; nor, when already a man, have chosen to be found in fashion as a man. He made those decisions as One already existing in the form of God (*en morphē theou huparchōn*). Of course the Lord also made decisions as a man, including the decision to adhere to his humiliation and enter more fully into its implications. This is made plain in verse 8: 'And being found in fashion as a man he humbled himself.' But of whom else would we need to be reminded that this decision, as contrasted with the earlier one, was taken when he was a man? The Lord's prior existence in the form of God was the pre-condition of his emptying himself, just as David's prior status as a prophet (*prophētēs huparchōn*) was the pre-condition of his making the utterance referred to in Acts 2:30.

But the contrast is not merely between two distinct phases in the Lord's existence. There is a contrast, too, between two distinct modes of being. Not that this is special to Philippians Two. It also occurs in John's Prologue (*theos* and *sarx*) and in 2 Corinthians 8:9 (being rich, becoming poor). In the Philippians passage, it is a contrast between the *form of God* and the *form of a servant*. The form of God is what he was: the participle *huparchōn* corresponds to John's imperfect tense, 'the Word *was* (*ēn*) God.' The form of a servant is what he *took* (corresponding to John's 'he *became* flesh'). The contrast between these two states is such that for Christ to take the form of a servant (*morphēn doulou*) was the supreme act of selflessness. To become a man was to make himself nothing.

But if the *form of God* is contrasted with the *form of a servant* it is parallel to *equal with God*. There is, of course, debate as to whether this equality was merely an option that Christ did not clutch at, or something already possessed that he did not cling to. There is nothing in the word *harpagmon*, which occurs only here in the New Testament, to preclude the latter interpretation. Bearing in mind that the reference is to the pre-existent state, that the New Testament does not scruple to call him *God* and that he is the *image* and *glory* of God, there is every justification for taking Christ's being equal with God as something which was true of him before he became incarnate. The implications of the idea are clear from John 5:18: 'This was why the Jews sought to kill him, because he not only broke the Sabbath but also called God his own Father, making himself equal with God.' The Jews clearly understood the assertion of equality with God to be blasphemous. It is worth noting, however, that in John 5:18 the word *equal* is

singular (*ison*) whereas in Philippians 2:6 it is plural (*isa*).
Lightfoot[33] points out that it was neither the Lord himself nor the
Evangelist who made the statement recorded in John. It was the
Jews. On the other hand, neither the Lord nor John repudiates it.
It may be unwise to read too much into the distinction between
the singular and the plural but certainly, if there is a difference in
nuance, it cannot be expressed better than by Lightfoot himself:
'Between the two expressions *isos einai* and *isa einai* no other
distinction can be drawn, except that the former refers to the
person, the latter to the *attributes*.' If this is so, then what Paul is
pointing to in Philippians 2:6 is equality in attributes between
God and Christ.

That the phrase *en morphē theou* points to a pre-existent
divine state is also clear from the conclusion to the hymn. In verse
9 we are told that God has not only highly (or *hyper*) exalted him
but has given him the name above every name. This can be no
other than the sacred name, Jahweh: LORD in the fullest sense. If
further proof is needed it can be found in the quotation from Isaiah
45:23: 'Unto me every knee shall bow, every tongue shall swear.'
The original speaker is God himself, yet the writer of the hymn
applies the words to Christ not as a mere allusion, but so as to
indicate that in his view the hyper-exaltation of Jesus, conceived
of as Lord, was precisely what the Original Speaker had in mind.
The meaning of *morphē theou* must agree with this. It is difficult
to believe that Paul could ascribe the name Jahweh (and the
worship that goes along with it) to one who was less or other than
God.

Last Adam Christology

A radically different approach to Philippians 2:6-11 has been taken
by some of those scholars who set it within the framework of a
Last Adam Christology. James D.G. Dunn is a typical example:
'It seems to me that Philippians 2:6-11 is best understood as an
expression of Adam Christology, one of the fullest expressions
that we still possess.'[34] This implies, in general, that the passage
is heavily influenced by Genesis 1–3. The *form of God* 'probably
refers' to Adam having been made in the image of God and with

a share of the glory of God. The *form of a servant* 'probably refers therefore' to what Adam became as a result of his fall. He lost his share in God's glory and became a slave. *Equality with God* 'probably alludes' to Adam's temptation. He was tempted by the promise, 'Ye shall be as god(s)', grasped at it and fell. Christ, by contrast, did not grasp at being equal. Instead, he chose to empty himself of Adam's glory and to share the lot into which Adam had fallen as a punishment for his sin. He made himself powerless (*heauton ekenōsen*), took the form of a slave and the likeness of men and came to share fully in mankind's mortality and corruption.

One consequence of this approach is that we can eliminate from the passage all ideas of pre-existence. Dunn lays down an extraordinary principle: 'The terms used in the passage do not have an independent value: *their sense is determined by their role within the Adam Christology*, by their function in describing Adam, or more generally God's purpose for man.'[35] The First Adam was not pre-existent. Therefore Christ, the Last Adam, was not pre-existent: 'The initial stage of Christ's odyssey is depicted as equivalent to Adam's status and choice in the garden.... So no implication that Christ was pre-existent may be intended. If Christ walks in Adam's footsteps then Christ need be no more pre-existent than Adam.'[36]

There are very serious difficulties, however, in imposing this model, impressive though it is, on Philippians 2:6-11. To begin with the most obvious point, the key-phrase, *en morphē theou*, does not occur in Genesis One at all. What does occur there (*image* and *likeness*) is, as we have seen, closely related to it. But it is highly doubtful whether readers working within the first-century context of meaning (to use Dunn's own concept) would have recognised the word *form* as a signal to start thinking about Adam.

Furthermore, Dunn's interpretation disjoins *en morphē theou* from *isa theō*. The one (being in the form of God) was already in the Lord's possession. The other (being equal with God) was not. It was only something he was tempted to grasp at. In fact, for Dunn this becomes the whole point of the analogy. Unlike Adam, Christ did not succumb to the temptation, 'Ye shall be as god(s).' However, if the exegesis we have argued for above is correct, then the form of God is synonymous with the glory of God and the fullness of God, and as such carried with it the idea of being equal with God. Christ as the *Shekinah* already has equality with God. There could not therefore have been for him any temptation to grasp at it.

The Adam Christology also requires a re-interpretation of *kenosis*. It no longer means Christ foregoing something he had. It means only his deciding not to grasp at something he did not have. This is certainly impressive enough, but not when compared with the *kenosis* Paul envisages in 2 Corinthians 8:9. According to this passage the Christ who enjoyed a pre-existent state where he was 'rich beyond all splendour' chose a temporal state of the deepest poverty. This is surely the idea best suited to the context of Philippians 2:6. The problem at Philippi was not people grasping at what they did not possess but believers vainly glorying in what they had. They were standing on their rights and asserting their dignity. Each knew what he was and wanted others to know it, too. They clung to every scrap of glory. They thought only of themselves. Christ, by contrast, laid his glory aside and took another *morphē*. He appeared without any of the accoutrements and insignia of greatness, content to appear a mere man.

Finally, what, on Dunn's interpretation, are we to make of the phrase, 'being found in fashion as a man'? When, in terms of the Adam Christology, was he ever anything else? His whole existence, on this construction, was confined to the flesh and the *kenosis* itself was only a lower form of fleshly existence than he might have grasped at. On such a view, there was no need for the resumptive phrase, 'being found in a fashion as a man.' When was he not man? When was he not flesh? When, in his earthly life, was he not weak and poor?

If the original *kenosis* was the result of a pre-temporal decision, however, this phrase makes good sense. It highlights the human existence as something remarkable in itself and it reminds us that the humiliation was not over with the mere assumption of the servant's form. In that form, as one fully involved in the human condition, he makes another decision: indeed a series of decisions. He decides to humble himself further, to go lower than Bethlehem, to go down *via* Nazareth, Galilee and Gethsemane to Calvary.

There is, of course, a legitimate Last Adam Christology, one which is quite consistent with the traditional interpretation of Philippians 2:6-11. We find it, for example, in Romans 5:12 ff., where the two Adams are compared and contrasted. Adam is a type of Christ to the extent that he is a representative figure, whose actions involve traumatic consequences for the many. But the main emphasis is on contrast: obedience against disobedience, justification against condemnation, life against death.

We find the Last Adam Christology again in 1 Corinthians 15:22, 45 and 47. But here, too, the main emphasis is on the contrast between the First Adam and the Last: 'As in Adam all *die*, so in Christ shall all be made *alive*': 'The first man Adam became a *living* creature (*psuchēn zōsan*). The last Adam a *life-giving* spirit': 'The first man is of the *earth, earthy*: the second man is the Lord *from heaven.*' This last reference is notable for another reason, too. The Last Adam is the Lord: and he is from heaven. In the face of such a statement it is difficult to maintain that in the New Testament the Last Adam Christology does not involve the ideas of pre-existence and divine lordship.

Nor is the Last Adam perspective confined to the Pauline writings. We find echoes of it, too, in the Epistle to the Hebrews, especially in chapter 2:5-9. This passage, though a quotation from Psalm 8, is referring to the creation narrative in which the Son of Man (Adam) is given dominion over the world to come. In accordance with this, dominion over the world (*oikoumenēn*) to come is given to Jesus. The mandate to the First Adam to subdue the earth is fulfilled in Christ as the Last Adam and the Son of Man. God has crowned him with glory and honour. He is the King of Creation. But what was the prelude and precondition of this exaltation? That he tasted death for every man! It was on account of that that he was crowned. But this completely breaks the Last Adam mould. There is no reference in the Genesis narrative to death as the road to supremacy. Furthermore, true though it is that Christ was made 'a little lower than the angels', this cannot be interpreted in isolation from the teaching of the earlier part of the Epistle, where Christ is said to have been made 'so much better than the angels'. He is uniquely a Son, the brightness of the Father's glory and the express image of his being. The idea that a Last Adam Christology could not transcend its original setting is surely fractured by the whole context of Hebrews 2:5-9. The Last Adam is something the Lord *became*, when he laid hold of the seed of Abraham (verse 16). It was far from being the whole truth. He knew a prior existence as the Son of God, and as Creator and Sustainer of the universe. And he knows a post-existence not only as Man, experiencing divinely promised fulfilment as Subjugator of the world, but as God's Equal, sitting at the right hand of 'the majesty on high'.

It is noteworthy that in all these Last Adam passages the New Testament focuses not on the existential side of the Lord's existence but on the eschatological. In Romans 5, he brings righteousness and life. In 1 Corinthians 15, he is life-giving Spirit. In Hebrews, he is Regnant Man, the King of Creation. At no point is the Adam parallel referred to the Lord's human-decision-making. This omission is especially noteworthy with regard to the temptations. This was the obvious point for the early church to introduce Adam. But it doesn't. There is no Garden. There is no Serpent. There is none of the language of Genesis 3. In fact, in Genesis it was Eve, not Adam, who was tempted and it was to her that the possibility of being like God was put. And when her motivation is analysed, it is not analysed at all in terms of *kenosis* and its alternative. She is said to have taken the fruit not because she had aspirations to deity but for three much more mundane reasons: it was good for food, it was pleasant to the eyes and it made one wise (Gen. 3:6). As for Adam, far from being portrayed as rejecting *kenosis* or aspiring to deity the whole truth is summed up in the terse statement: 'she gave also unto her husband with her, and he did eat.'

Dunn seems to have locked himself into an impossible hermeneutic. It is perilous to assume that if a writer uses a word or two which also occurs in an Old Testament narrative he is invoking the whole of that narrative. In the present instance, it is as if the word *morphē* were a password which gave access to a whole new programme on our exegetical computer (and, of course, cancelled all previous programmes). We are asked to believe that the occurrence of this one word indicates that the writer of Philippians 2 is not only thinking of Genesis 3 but is thinking *within* it: we cannot introduce into the New Testament passage any ideas which were not obviously implicit in the Old. Nothing can be affirmed of the Last Adam which was not affirmed of the First. Dunn says so explicitly, in words already quoted: 'The terms used in the passage do not have an independent value; their sense is determined by their role within the Adam Christology, by their function in describing Adam, or more generally God's purpose for men.'[37]

Are we to impose similar constraints on every designation applied to Christ? For example, when we read that he was Son of David, does that mean that we are to ascribe to him nothing that was not also true of the original David? When we read that he was *God*, are we to say to ourselves that we must not read into that any more than *theos* meant to the Greeks, *deus* to the Romans and *allah* to the Semitic peoples generally? This is to repeat on a larger scale the classic semantic fallacy of regarding etymology as decisive for the meaning of words. We cannot deduce the meaning of *nice* from the fact that it is derived from the Latin *nescius*, meaning *ignorant*. And we cannot ascertain the meaning of the designation *the Last Adam* by tracing it to its origin in Genesis and concluding that its original meaning must be forever its true one.

It is interesting to ponder how Dunn's own writings would fare if subjected to such a hermeneutic. For example, at one point he writes that 'the initial stage of Christ's *odyssey* is depicted as equivalent to Adam's status and choice in the garden'.[38] What would we think of some future researcher writing a thesis on Dunn and concluding from this phrase that he held to a *Ulysses* Christology: and not only so, but refusing to ascribe to Dunn's Christ anything which was not also true of Ulysses? Or to descend to an even lower plain: it is almost inevitable that some preacher, somewhere, has referred to Christ as 'the greatest'. Does that mean that he held to a Muhammed Ali Christology? That he was applying to Christ all that was true of the boxer? And nothing that was not true of the boxer?

That may seem absurd. But is it any more so than some of the methods currently in vogue among New Testament scholars? It might be helpful to ask, now and again, Does anyone interpret any other literature like this? Do English scholars insist that Shakespeare's *Hamlet* and *Macbeth* can rise no higher than their originals? It might even help us to ask, 'How would I feel if this kind of interpretation were applied to *my* letters, *my* books and *my* sermons?' Paul sure would be surprised if he could come back today to benefit from the wisdom of his exegetes, all longing to tell him where he got his language from, all insisting that whenever he used a word he was thinking of everything associated with it, and all convinced that he never enriched a word by the addition of a new idea.

To imagine that when Paul wrote (or used) Philippians 2:6-11 he had in mind every Old Testament allusion to Adam is to engage in what would be called in semantics 'illegitimate totality transfer'. To argue that his thought could rise no higher than its Old Testament source is blatant reductionism.

Three other objections to the Last Adam Christology (at least in this form) may be mentioned briefly.

First, its advocates refuse to be specific on crucial matters of detail. The most important point in the alleged parallel is that Christ, like Adam, made a choice. The one chose to grasp at being equal with God: the other chose not to. As we have already seen, in the Genesis narrative Adam made no such choice. It was Eve who made it. But that detail apart, when did Christ make such a choice? Where in his earthly life is the point of *kenosis*? Dunn himself is aware of the question: 'In what sense or when was the earthly Jesus confronted with a choice as archetypal as Adam's – in childhood, at Jordan, in the wilderness, at Caesarea Philippi?'[39] He gives a fascinating answer: 'To press this question is probably once again to misunderstand what this hymn is trying to do. It does not seek to narrate a particular event or temptation as such, but simply describes in Adam language *the character of Christ's whole life*' (italics his). But this will not do. Even if his whole life *was* a temptation to grasp at equality with God, this must have out-cropped in particular critical episodes. Furthermore, we are supposed to be focusing on an Adam-Christ parallel. For Adam the choice was not spread over a life-time. It was condensed into one decisive moment. Besides, it bifurcated Adam's existence into a pre-choice and a post-choice phase. That parallel can be preserved by the traditional interpretation of Philippians 2:5-11: Christ had a *pre-kenosis* and a *post-kenosis* existence. On Dunn's interpretation this is impossible. Nowhere in the Lord's earthly life can we draw the line between the form of God and the form of a servant; or between his being rich and his becoming poor (2 Cor. 8:9).

Secondly, there are marked differences between the Bible's portrayal of Adam as image-bearer and its portrayal of Christ as image-bearer. It is quite impossible to apply to Adam or any of his natural descendants the kind of language applied to Christ in Colossians 1:15 ff., according to which he created all things, he upholds all things, he owns all things, he was before all things, and he is pre-eminent over all things; all because in him there dwells the *plēroma* of God. It is equally impossible to apply to Adam the language of Hebrews 1:3, to the effect that Christ is the brightness of the Father's glory and the express image of his being and upholds all things by the word of his power. Whether we talk in terms of being or in terms of function the Last Adam has 'a glory that excelleth'. Indeed, had Christ been no more than Adam he could not have served God's redemptive purpose. 'The power of the atoning act must be greater than the power of sin,' writes Oscar Cullmann: 'A single spark is enough to set a whole forest on fire, but infinitely greater power is required to extinguish the fire. In the case of the Second Adam's atoning work, one individual brings also this greater power.'[40]

Finally, there is nothing in the story of Adam corresponding to the climax of the Christ-hymn in Philippians 2: 'Wherefore God also hyper-exalted him and gave him the Name which is above every name: that at the Name of Jesus every knee should bow in heaven and earth and under the earth and every tongue confess that Jesus Christ is *Lord*, to the glory of God the Father.' At the heart of this passage lies a quotation from Isaiah 45:22-23: 'Look unto me and be ye saved, all the ends of the earth; for I am God, and there is none else. I have sworn by myself, the word is gone

out of my mouth in righteousness and shall not return. Unto me
every knee shall bow, every tongue shall swear.' Dunn is aware
of the difficulty which this ascription to Christ of a passage
originally referring to Jahweh creates for his theory: 'Certainly
the use of the strongly monotheistic passage (Isaiah 45:23) adds a
new dimension to the Christological claim, but apart from that
the assertion of universal homage before Christ is simply the
obverse of the assertion of the universal sovereignty of Christ.'[41]
This sentence is masterly in its equivocation, but when all is said
and done the assertion of universal homage rests in the hymn not
on the fact that Christ is the Last Adam but on the fact that he is
Lord. As the affirmation climaxes, Christ is being worshipped by
the church, adored by the angels and dreaded by the demons: and
the passage of Scripture suggested by the association of ideas is
not Genesis 3 but Matthew 4:10, 'Thou shalt worship the Lord
thy God, and him only shalt thou serve.'

   There is a large measure of arbitrariness in describing
Philippians 2:5-11 as an example of Last Adam Christology. It
could be described with at least equal accuracy as an example of
Servant Christology or of *Kurios* Christology. These ideas are
just as prominent as the Last Adam idea. In the last analysis, of
course, it does not matter what kind of Christology we call it, so
long as we do justice to the teaching itself. Unfortunately, it is all
too easy to imagine that once we have found a suitable pigeon-
hole we have grasped the message. More unfortunately still, some
scholars have turned their category into a strait-jacket. The *form*,
the *kenosis* and the very *lordship* itself have to be shrunk to fit
into the Adam-mould. This is simply inadmissible. Adam, indeed,
is here. But then, so is the Servant; and so is the Lord. It is doubtful,
however, whether any of these is dominant. What we have here
pre-eminently is a *Shekinah* Christology. This is the form he
originally possessed. That is the glory he did not cling to. That is
the majesty he obscured on Calvary. And that is the reality which
supports the concluding protestation:

   At the Name of Jesus
   Every knee shall bow,

Every tongue confess Him
King of glory now.
'Tis the Father's pleasure
We should call Him Lord,
Who from the beginning
Was the mighty Word.

Conclusion

There appears to be little room for doubt that the New Testament designates Jesus *God* and describes him as the divine image, form and glory. At the most obvious (and important) level these are statements about Jesus. They ascribe to him the status of deity. They proclaim that he possesses the attributes, exercises the prerogatives and performs the functions of God; and by doing this they lay the foundations for Christian worship, directed specifically to Christ as Lord.

But there is another level of truth here, almost equally important. These are not merely statements about Jesus. They are also statements about God: about the very nature of deity itself. They not only predicate deity of Jesus. They also predicate Jesus-ness or Christ-likeness of deity. In God, there is no un-Christ-likeness at all. In Christ, we see God's very nature. Christ is God's definition and explanation of himself, so that we may read off from Jesus the deepest truths about deity itself.

The implications of this are momentous, not least because they cut across our human expectations and presuppositions. Our whole instinct is to conceive of God primarily in terms of awe and power. This is suggested in the general Semitic designations for God (*El* and its derivations) and in the universal concern with piacular religion. It is also reflected in Paul's philosophy of religion as described in Romans 1:18-32. What all men see clearly is 'the eternal power and godhead' of God and what is impressed indelibly on their consciences is the knowledge of the judgement of God. Even within Christianity, centuries of conditioning have led us to think of God primarily in terms of rectitude, dominion and wrath. The revelation given in Christ does not eliminate these. But it does bring a profound change of emphasis. It remains a revelation of glory, but the glory is no longer primarily a consuming fire. It is a glory full of grace and truth. We see the form of a servant. We see One who while still existing only in the form of God chose not to cling to status or to stand on his dignity. It is the very form of God not to look on his own things but on the things of others. The impulse to serve and to take the road to the Cross comes from deep within God himself, is fully consonant with his nature and gives supreme and definitive expression to his essence.

How all this looks to human eyes is clear from the words of Peter in John 13:8, 'Thou shalt never wash my feet.' It is the very nature of Jesus (and of the God we see in him) to wash disciples' feet. But this offends all our human expectations. Man expects God to be like himself. If man had power and dominion he would look to his own things, not to the things of others. To make matters worse, the foot-washing is only a beginning. The paradox culminates on Calvary. Here is the final self-emptying and the final self-obscuring of God. Yet here, too, is the final revelation and the final self-fulfilment of God. Here he proclaims himself *love*: such love that he gave himself and (what is even deeper) gave his Son. The place of shame and darkness and pain, where the Most High is most completely veiled, becomes the place where he is most completely un-veiled. Where he most unequivocably serves, he is most unequivocally Lord. And yet, startling though that is, it does not go beyond the expectation of the Old Testament: 'Who is a God like thee, who pardons iniquity and passes by the transgression of the remnant of his heritage?' (Micah 7:18). In this, he is most Other: in Pardon, Love and Service.

The one point it may be appropriate to add is that Jesus is *uniquely* the revelation of God. He is *the* image and *the* glory just as he is *the* way, *the* truth and *the* life: 'No man knows the Father except the Son and whoever the Son decides to reveal him to' (Matt. 11:27).

We must interpret this with some care, however. There was revelation in the Old Testament and there was (and continues to be) revelation 'through the things that are made' (Rom. 1:20). But both were connected with Christ. He was the author of the

Old Testament revelation insofar as it was his Spirit that spoke in the prophets (1 Pet. 1:11). It was also of him that that revelation spoke (1 Pet. 1:11; Luke 24:27). The same is true of the revelation given through creation. The world was made by the Logos. He is its Logic and Wisdom and when we behold it it is his glory we see. In the Old Testament and in General Revelation alike, Christ is both the Revealer and the Revealed. But this climaxes in his mission when he reveals himself not merely in intermittent eruptions and occasional prophecies but in his personal and visible presence and (the supreme moment of divine self-disclosure) on the Cross.

Those who know neither the incarnation nor Calvary are not entirely ignorant of God. All men know his 'eternal power and godhood' (Rom. 1:20) and some also derive additional light from the Old Testament. But they do not know the Mystery: that God is Love. They have not seen the Glory: God in Servant's form. They do not know the Way and this precludes them from walking in it. The divine Word is both exclusivist (there is no other Name) and judgemental (on other religions). But it was not meant to end in either of these. It was meant to end in evangelism. Those who sat in darkness have seen a great light.

References

1. V. Taylor, "Does the New Testament Call Jesus God?" *(Expository Times,* Vol. LXIII, No 4, January 1962, pp.116-118).

2. M. R. Austin, "Salvation and the Divinity of Jesus" (*Expository Times,* Vol.96, No. 9, June 1985, pp.271-275).

3. R. Bultmann, *The Theology of the New Testament* (London: SCM Press, 1965), Vol. 1, p.129.

4. D. Cupitt, *The Debate about Christ* (London: SCM Press, 1979), p.91.

5. N. Turner, *Grammatical Insights into the New Testament* (Edinburgh: T&T Clark, 1965), p.17.

6. G.H.C. Macgregor, *The Gospel of John* (London: Hodder & Stoughton, 1928, p.4.

7. B.F. Westcott, *The Gospel according to St John* (London: John Murray, 1896), p.3.

8. E.C. Hoskyns, *The Fourth Gospel* (London: Faber & Faber, Second Edition revised, 1947), p.154.

9. C.K. Barrett, *The Gospel according to St John* (London: SPCK, 1960), p.141.

10. B.F. Westcott, *The Epistle to the Hebrews* (London: Macmillan, 1889), p.25.

11. N. Turner, *Grammatical Insights into the New Testament*, p.15.

12. F.F. Bruce, *Commentary on the Epistle to the Hebrews* (London: Marshall, Morgan and Scott, 1965), p.19.

13. F. Young in J. Hick (Ed.), *The Myth of God Incarnate* (London: SCM Press, 1977), p.21.

14. C. H. Dodd, *The Epistle of Paul to the Romans* (London: Collins [Fontana Books], 1959), p.165.

15. C.A. Anderson Scott, *Christianity According to St Paul* (Cambridge: Cambridge University Press, 1966), p. 273.

16. R. Bultmann, *The Theology of the New Testament*, Vol. I, p. 129.

17. W. Sanday & A.C. Headlam, *The Epistle of Paul to the Romans* (Edinburgh: T & T Clark, 5th edition, 1902), p. 233.

18. Athanasius, *Against the Arians*, I.10 (Nicene and Post-Nicene Fathers [New Edition, Grand Rapids, Eerdmans, 1957] Vol. IV, p. 311.

19. Augustine, *On the Trinity*, Bk. II, Chap. 13 (Nicene and Post-Nicene Fathers, Vol. III, p. 48).

20. O. Cullmann, *The Christology of the New Testament* (London: SCM Press, Second Edition, 1963), p. 313.

21. C.H. Dodd, *The Epistle of Paul to the Romans*, p. 165.

22. The only question is whether the words were in fact written by Paul or, with the other Pastoral Epistles, by some pseudonymous author. But that problem lies beyond our remit.

23. N. Turner, *Grammatical Insights into the New Testament*, p. 16.

24. A.T. Robertson, *A Grammar of the Greek New Testament* (New York: Hodder & Stoughton, Third Edition, 1919), p. 786.

25. H. Montefiore, *A Commentary on the Epistle to the Hebrews* (London: A & C Black, 1964), p. 47.

26. J.B. Lightfoot, *Saint Paul's Epistle to the Philippians*, (London: Macmillan, Fourth Edition, 1879), p. 127.

27. B.B. Warfield, *The Person and Work of Christ* (Philadelphia: Presbyterian and Reformed, 1950), p. 39.

28. R.P. Martin, *Carmen Christi* (Cambridge: Cambridge University Press, 1967), pp. 99-133.

29. J.B. Lightfoot, *St. Paul's Epistles to the Colossians and to Philemon* (London: Macmillan, Eighth Edition, 1886), p. 156.

30. F.J.A. Hort, *The Epistle of St. James* (London: Macmillan, 1909), p. 47.

31. J.B. Mayor, *The Epistle of St. James* (London: Macmillan, 1982) p. 75.

32. A.T. Hanson, *Grace and Truth: A Study in the Doctrine of the Incarnation* (London: SPCK, 1975), pp.5-9.

33. J.B. Lightfoot, *Saint Paul's Epistle to the Philippians*, p. 112.

34. J.D.G. Dunn, *Christology in the Making* (London: SCM Press, 1980), p. 114.

35. Dunn, *op. cit.,* p. 119.

36. Dunn, *ibid.*

37. Dunn, *ibid.*

38. Dunn, *ibid.*

39. Dunn, *op. cit.*, p.120.

40. O. Cullmann, *The Christology of the New Testament*, p. 173.

41. J.D.G. Dunn, *Christology in the Making*, p. 118.

2

JESUS IS LORD

To the modern Christian in search of biblical support for his belief in the deity of Christ the supremely important thing is that the New Testament specifically calls him *God (theos)*. As Oscar Cullmann points out, however, 'This name by no means indicates, as we are inclined to think, a higher dignity than the unsurpassable *kurios* designation.'[1]

The name itself has been the focus of considerable critical attention. In a famous study entitled *Kurios Christos* (first published in 1913) William Bousset argued that the title was not applied to Jesus by the original, Aramaic-speaking Christians but arose in the Greek-speaking churches of Damascus and Antioch. Rudolf Bultmann held substantially the same opinion: the title was derived from the religious terminology of Hellenism.[2]

But this theory is now discredited. It was vulnerable on three counts.

First, there was the evidence of the early preaching in Acts, where Christ is frequently referred to as *kurios*, especially in the combination *Lord Jesus* (Acts 2:36; 5:14; 8:16; 9:5). Even if we were to admit that these are not verbally accurate reports of actual preaching it would remain that the early chapters of Acts are clearly based on a Hebraistic source and represent the attitudes and nomenclature of the pre-Pauline community.

Secondly, there was the attitude of James. This was especially important because of his unique position. James' Epistle is one of the earliest (and possibly the very earliest) of the New Testament documents, dating from the fifth decade of the first century. He himself was thoroughly rooted in the Aramaic-speaking Jewish community. Indeed, he was a prominent figure who commanded the respect even of non-Christians and earned the appellation 'James the Just' on account of his respect for the Law. In Acts Fifteen he has already emerged as the clear leader of the Jerusalem church. Most important of all, he was Jesus' brother. It is surely very impressive, in the light of these considerations, that in the opening words of his epistle he refers to Christ as *Lord*: 'James, a servant of God and of the Lord Jesus Christ.' He repeats the designation in the remarkable words we have already seen at the beginning of his second chapter: 'My brethren, show no partiality as you hold the faith of our Lord Jesus Christ, the Glory.' It occurs yet again in James 5:7: 'Be patient, therefore, until the coming of the Lord.' James is the archetypal exponent of Jewish Christianity and his usage makes it virtually certain that the designation *kurios* was prevalent among Christians from the very beginning.

Thirdly, there was the liturgical formula *Marana tha*, which occurs in 1 Corinthians 16:22. This is what A.E.J. Rawlinson called, in a famous phrase, 'the Achilles' heel of Bousset's theory.'[3] This is the earliest Christian liturgical formula extant. It is Aramaic: and it invokes Jesus as *mar* (Lord). The exact meaning of the words is not absolutely certain.[4] They may be read *maran atha* ('Our Lord comes!') or *marana tha* ('Our Lord, come!'). Two things favour the latter reading. First, a prayer is more likely to have been preserved in its original form than a theological proposition. Secondly, there is another instance of the prayer, 'Come, Lord!' elsewhere in the New Testament, namely in Revelation 22:20 (*Erchou, kurie Iesou*). This seems decisive in favour of taking 1 Corinthians 16:22 in the same sense.

In the abstract, the title *mar* may mean no more than *didaskale* (teacher). But as C.F.D. Moule points out, 'One does not call on a mere Rabbi, after his death, to come. The entire phrase would be bound to carry transcendental overtones even if the *MARAN* by itself did not.'[5]

But even if the title does go back to the earliest, Aramaic-speaking Christians, does it also go back to Christ? Does it reflect *his* self-understanding, or even agree with it?

The distribution of the *kurios* title in the Synoptics is certainly remarkable. Luke uses it in his narrative at four points. The earliest occurrence is in the words of Elizabeth to Mary: 'And why is this granted me, that the mother of my Lord should come to me?' (Luke 1:43). It occurs again in Luke 2:11: 'For unto you is born this day in the city of David a Saviour, who is Christ the Lord.'

Peter uses the vocative form (*kurie*) in his response to Christ in Luke 5:8: 'Depart from me, for I am a sinful man, O Lord.' The translation of 'Sir' is hardly adequate here. Peter's exclamation has been evoked by the miraculous draught of fishes and he is prostrate before Christ as he utters it, overwhelmed with a sense of creatureliness and sin. In Luke 24:34 the title *kurios* is used absolutely: 'The Lord has risen indeed and has appeared to Simon.'

Matthew and Mark, by contrast, do not use the title in their narrative at all. This (along with the scarcity of the title in Luke) is probably an accurate reflection of the historical situation: Christ was seldom designated *kurios* during his lifetime. This is all the more remarkable in view of the fact that in the Book of Acts and in the Epistles the title abounds. The only factor available to account for the change is the Resurrection. This event did not change the status of Christ, but it certainly did change the disciples' perception of him.

It is interesting, too, to contrast the distribution of the title *kurios* with the title *Son of Man*. The latter abounds on the lips of Jesus, yet never occurs in the usage of the early church. The former abounds in the early church, yet is seldom found on the lips of the Saviour. This is not to say, however, that the later usage is entirely unwarranted by Christ's own practice. The title *kurios* is used several times by the Christ of the Synoptic Gospels.

The earliest occurrence is in Mark 2:28: 'The Son of Man is Lord of the Sabbath.' Here, *kurios* may be functional: 'the Son of Man has lordship over the Sabbath.' Even so, the claim is a bold one. God in the Old Testament had referred to the Sabbath as 'my Sabbath' (Isa. 56:4). Now Christ, at a very early stage in his ministry, is claiming it as his: and claiming the right to declare, in his own name, how it should be observed. In view of these considerations the question whether the title is functional or ontic is rather irrelevant.

It occurs again in Matthew 7:21, 22: 'Not every one who says to me, *kurie, kurie*, shall enter the kingdom of heaven.... On that day, many will say to me, *kurie, kurie*, did we not prophesy in your name and cast out demons in your name and do many mighty works in your name?' Once more, the context makes clear that

the vocative cannot be reduced to *Sir*! The *kurios* here is the
Judge, presiding at the Great Assize, and his name is of such
eminence that the people appearing before him have invoked it
(successfully) in the performance of miracles. His authority is
ultimate and his word final: 'I will declare to them, "I never knew
you; depart from me, you workers of evil!" '

There is an even more interesting occurrence of *kurios* in
Matthew 22:41 ff. Here the Lord is putting to the Pharisees the
specific question, 'Whose son is Christ?' They reply, 'The Son of
David!' and Jesus, by way of rejoinder, quotes Psalm 110:1, 'The
Lord said to my Lord (Jehovah said to Adonai).' Christ focuses
on the precise meaning of *adonai, My* Lord: 'If David calls the
Messiah his Lord, how can he be his Son?'

It seems fair to conclude that the title *kurios* was applied to
Christ by the Christian community from the very beginning; and
that this usage was suggested by the occasional practice of Christ
himself. After the resurrection it became the most common of all
titles for the Saviour. It involved at least four great ideas.

First, *ownership*, particularly the ownership of slaves. This idea
was reinforced by the occasional application to Christ of the title
despotēs, suggesting absolute dominion, without restraints. We
find this title, for example, in 2 Peter 2:1: 'There will be false
teachers among you, who will secretly bring in destructive heresies,
even denying the *despotēs* who bought them.' It also occurs in
Jude 4: 'Admission has been gained by ungodly persons who deny
our only *despotēs* and *kurios*, Jesus Christ.' Corresponding to
this is the frequent description of Christians, including the apostles,
as slaves (*douloi*) of Christ. In serving their fellowmen they were
diakonoi: in serving Christ, they were *douloi*. Furthermore, this
serving of Jesus was symmetrical with serving God: James was
the *doulos* of God and of the Lord Jesus Christ (Jas. 1:1). This
kind of language would surely have been impossible unless Christ
had a status commensurate with God's. The corollary to this was
the sense of unconditional obligation imposed by Christ. We are
to forsake all and follow him, even though this means leaving our
dead unburied, forsaking houses and lands, abandoning fathers
and mothers, brothers and sisters, and, at last, taking up our crosses

and laying down our lives (Mark 8:34; 10:29; Matt. 10:37; Luke 9:60). His demand takes precedence over all other commitments. In his word, we meet categorical imperative.

Yet this Master-Servant relationship has a curious polarity in the New Testament. The Lord himself comes in the form of a servant (*doulos*) and is among us as One who serves (*diakonos*). Indeed, service was precisely what he came for and an extraordinary service it was, too: to lay down his life as a ransom for many (Mark 10:45). Conversely, Christians are not only servants but also lords. As sons of God and heirs of God all things are theirs (1 Cor. 3:21) and angels minister to them (Heb. 1:14). This is already true in the present and will be even more true in the future. One day, man in Christ will find the destiny planned for him in Genesis 1:26. He will be Lord of Creation.

The second idea associated with *kurios* is *teaching*. It is interesting that the vocative *kurie* in Matthew's account of the Transfiguration (Matt. 17:4) is represented by *Rabbi* in Mark (9:5). It is even more interesting that 'in the Gospel of Mark there is only a single example of the *kurie* form of address, that by the Syro-Phoenician woman; in all other instances *didaskale* is used.'[6] *kurie, rabbi* and *didaskale* were clearly interchangeable translations of an underlying Aramaic, although there is some evidence that Matthew in particular had scruples about putting the invocation *kurie* on the lips of those who were less than true disciples. For example, at the Supper, while the eleven address Christ as *kurie*, Judas calls him *didaskale* (Matt. 26:22, 25). 'It is·plain then,' writes Vos, 'that the gospel writers were guided in this matter by the principle that the address *kurie* would have been less fitting in the mouth of certain people.'[7] It remains, however, that there was a close association between *kurios* and teaching. The teacher was an authority-figure. The root meaning of *rabbi* (from *rab*) was 'the great one' and the reason for forbidding women to teach was that such a role involved exercising authority over men (1 Tim. 2:12). Yet Jesus was no ordinary teacher, precisely because unlike the Scribes, he taught with authority. That assessment is recorded, of course, immediately after the Sermon on the Mount (Matt. 7:29) in which Jesus showed his authority in a remarkable way. In particular, he had taught in his own name without appeal to any higher authority. He did not, like the rabbis, appeal to his predecessors (in fact, he explicitly contradicted the teaching of 'the ancients'). Nor had he, like the prophets, introduced his teaching with the formula, 'Thus saith the Lord.' He repudiated, innovated, clarified and stipulated in his own name: '*I* say to you.'

Important as the teaching ministry was during the earthly sojourn of Christ, however, it was overshadowed by the teaching activity of the risen Lord. Paul can of course quote the sayings of the earthly ministry when the occasion demands. He does so, for example, in 1 Corinthians 7:10: 'To the married I give charge, not I but the Lord, that the wife should not separate from her husband.' He does it again in 1 Thessalonians 4:15: 'This we declare unto you by the word of the Lord, that we who are left until the coming of the Lord shall not take precedence over those who have fallen asleep.' But what is particularly interesting is the apostolic attitude to Christ as the ultimate source of tradition. 'The designation *kurios*,' writes Oscar Cullmann, 'can be understood as not only pointing to the historical Jesus as the chronological beginning and the first link of the chain of tradition, but to the exalted Lord as the real author of the whole tradition developing itself within the apostolic church.... The risen Christ is himself the author of the gospel, of which he is also the object. He is both subject and object.'[8] One of the clearest examples of this is in 1 Corinthians 11:23: 'I received from the Lord what I also delivered to you.' The result of this process was that the apostles had the mind of Christ (1 Cor. 2:16) and that what they taught amounted to 'commands of the Lord' (1 Cor. 14:37). We must remember, however, that the risen Lord's activity as teacher was not confined to objective instruction and revelation. There was also a ministry of inward illumination. This appears particularly clearly in the story of Lydia's conversion in Acts 16:14: 'The Lord opened her heart to give heed to the things which were preached by Paul.'

Thirdly, lordship involves *authority*: not merely authority as a teacher but authority in the sense of *imperium*. This is linked to a variety of other concepts. For example, Christ has cosmic authority.

He can claim that he has been given all authority in heaven and in earth (Matt. 28:18) and that he possesses authority over all flesh (John 17:2). He sits at the right hand of the majesty (Heb. 1:3) and even in the very midst of the throne (Rev. 7:17). Then there is the idea of headship. He is the Head of the Church (Eph. 5:23) and Head over all things for the church (Eph. 1:22). Then again, he has supremacy over the spiritual powers. He is the head of all rule and authority (Col. 2:10), having disarmed the principalities and powers (Col. 2:15). He has bound Satan (Matt. 12:29; Rev. 20:2) and it is he who detains in eternal chains those angels who did not keep to their God-given sphere (Jude 6).

Above all, however, *imperium* is linked to the idea of Christ as King. The concept is not prominent in the Pauline epistles but there are clear echoes of it. One such echo is 1 Corinthians 15:24: 'Then comes the end, when he delivers up the kingdom to God the Father.' Another is in Colossians 1:13: 'God delivered us from the dominion of the Darkness and transported us into the kingdom of his dear Son.' But if the idea is rare in the epistles, it abounds in the Synoptic Gospels, beginning with the Baptist's pronouncement, 'The Kingdom of God is at hand' (Matt. 3:2) and ending with the indictment on the cross, 'Jesus of Nazareth, the King of the Jews.' The Baptist's words indicate that the Kingdom is imminent, if indeed not already present: and it is imminent because in Christ the King is already here. He is the Lord come to his temple (Mal. 3:1; Mark 1:2). He is the King invading the territory of the Enemy to rescue his people and to inaugurate his reign. The insignia of the kingdom follow him: mighty acts, especially of healing and exorcism, which fill men with wonder and constitute God's attestation of the Messiah. On Calvary the King appears to be defeated. In fact, however, the cross is his supreme kingly act by which he destroyed the one who had the power of death (Heb. 2:14) and put the principalities and powers to an open shame. The resurrection is his investiture, when he is appointed Son of God 'with power' (Rom. 1:4) and takes his seat on the throne. The symbolism of the Session appears contradictory, but is really complementary. The Lamb *stands* (Acts 7:56) as One still supremely active (*Acts* is surely the Book of the Acts of the risen

Lord). He *sits* (Heb. 1:3) as one resting after finishing the decisive phase of his work; and he will stand again only to effect its consummation. Even his position on the throne is rich in symbolism. He is at the right hand of the Majesty as the one who enjoys special favour. But he also sits in the very midst of the throne (Rev. 7:17) as the one who is at the heart (and even *is* the heart) of the divine sovereignty. In him, the Sovereignty is defined as the sovereignty of Grace: the love which became incarnate in him, reigns. Yet we must remember that in this exaltation he is but returning to the glory he had with the Father before the world was (John 17:5). Christ's role at the heart of the Sovereignty did not begin with the Ascension. If the Word was eternally with the Father (John 1:1) then the Sovereign was never without his Son. The effect of this is to *Christologise* the Sovereignty in all its aspects. There cannot be in it any un-Christlikeness at all. This goes back to the very roots of 'the counsel of his will'. Christ is a party to foreordination, election, predestination and reprobation, all of which fully reflect his character as holy wisdom, power and love. He is also at the heart of God's providence, so that neither things present nor things to come can separate us from his love (Rom. 8:38 f.). And he is at the heart of the judgement likewise. We shall stand not only at the judgement-seat of God but at the judgement-seat of Christ (2 Cor. 5:10): His involvement a pledge that the whole process will reflect infinite integrity, compassion and understanding, as well as reluctance to condemn (Hos. 11:8).

At all these points we have the comfort of knowing that if we have seen Christ then we have seen the Sovereign. He is the Truth about the Government, the Exegesis of the Throne and the Meaning of the Decree. But the corollary must be true, too. What Christ represents and incarnates now has sovereignty, dominion and power. God's love in him is not fragile, vulnerable and indecisive. It is in a position of dominance. He can move heaven and earth for a man's salvation. Every demon is at the end of *his* chain. The great words of William Cowper bear their highest sense as applied to the enthroned Lamb:

Deep in unfathomable mines
Of never-failing skill
He treasures up His bright designs
And works His sovereign will.

That is the comfort of a church charged with an impossible task: 'Go! I am with you; and I have all the authority' (Matt. 28:18 ff.). It is the comfort, too, of a people facing an arduous history. How glorious it is that the Apocalypse begins with a vision of 'a throne and him that sits on it' (Rev. 4:2). Only after we have fortified our hearts with that are we asked to contemplate the plagues and the pestilences, the famines and the battles, the Serpent, the Beast and the Scarlet Woman.

But if Christ *came* as King, why the exaltation? We have seen that the church's perception of the lordship of Christ appears to have altered after the resurrection. But did the lordship itself undergo change as well? Matthew speaks of an authority *given* to Christ by the Father (Matt. 28:18). John conceives of the glorification as an act of the Father (John 17:1). Paul speaks of the resurrection as the point where Christ was appointed Son of God *with power* (Rom. 1:4). All these passages refer to the incarnate Christ and clearly indicate that after the resurrection he possesses energy, authority and glory which were not his before. On earth, he had a lordship in *kenosis*. It was restrained and veiled, although still capable of mighty acts (*dunameis*). Now it is untrammelled and hyper-exalted. The signs of this new phase of his lordship are the binding of Satan (Heb. 2:14; Rev. 20:2), the mission of the Paraklete (John 16:7), and the fact that his disciples perform greater miracles than he did himself (John 14:12). In all this, the complex event of resurrection represents a *perfecting* of the Saviour: 'being made perfect, he became the source of eternal salvation to all who obey him' (Heb. 5:9). Only in the resurrection does he come to be fully equipped as Mediator: equipped, that is, with compassion, victory, power, authority and, above all, a perfect and accepted sacrifice. He now has authority over all flesh. But the reason for his having it is precisely that he may give eternal life to as many as the Father has given him (John 17:2).

Here again, however, there is a two-way process: not only is
the incarnate Christ modified by the sovereignty, but the
sovereignty itself is modified by the incarnation, especially as
perfected in the cross and resurrection of Christ. In him, the
sovereignty, too, becomes flesh. The Sovereign becomes one who
has been Servant. He has learned obedience (Heb. 5:8) and can be
touched with the feeling of our infirmities (Heb. 4:15). The Great
Shepherd is himself a Lamb, with the profoundest understanding
of the experiences of his flock. That is the final guarantee of the
humaneness of history.

Finally, for all the cultural streams which flow through the
New Testament, *kurios* implied *deity*. The pagans called their
gods (including Caesar) *kurioi*. There is a clear echo of this in 1
Corinthians 8:5-6: 'For although there are many "gods" and many
"lords" yet for us there is one God, the Father, and one Lord,
Jesus Christ.' This implies that *god* and *lord* were synonymous
and that as far as Paul was concerned what the pagans claimed for
their *lords* was found authentically only in Jesus Christ. Aramaic-
speaking Jews, calling Jesus *mar*, would be aware that in their
Targums the title was applied to God as the equivalent of *adon*.
Above all, Greek-speaking Jews would know that in the Septuagint
kurios was the usual rendering of the sacred name *JHWH*. It may,
as Bultmann suggests,[9] be highly improbable that the ascription
of the title to Christ was consciously derived from the Septuagint.
But it seems indubitable that as applied to Jesus it has all the force
of *JHWH* or *adon* in the Old Testament. This appears especially
from what C.F.D. Moule calls 'the apparently arbitrary assumption
that anything belonging to God also belongs to Christ'.[10] In
particular, Old Testament passages which in their original context
clearly applied to Jahweh are in the New Testament applied
unequivocally to Christ. A typical example is Malachi 3:1: 'Behold
I send my messenger to prepare the way before me, and the Lord
whom you seek will suddenly come to his temple.' Mark 1:2
applies this passage, without comment, to Christ. He is the Lord
and John the Baptist is *his* Messenger. We find the same thing in
Acts 2:21 where Peter appeals for faith in Christ by quoting to his
audience the words of Joel 2:32: 'As many as call on the name of

the Lord shall be saved.' But even more striking is what we find in Philippians 2:9-11. There can be no doubt that in this context the primitive Christian confession, 'Jesus is Lord,' has the highest possible connotation. God, we are told, has given him the name which is above every name. That can mean only one thing: Jahweh. That is the name before which every knee is to bow. As if that were not enough, Paul recounts the exaltation in words quoted from an Old Testament passage where Jahweh is clearly talking about himself: 'As I live, saith Jahweh, unto me every knee shall bow, every tongue shall swear.' There is something, too, in Moule's contention[11] that the Christology is so exalted that special care has to be taken to safeguard the supremacy of God. This may be why the phrase 'to the glory of God the Father' is inserted in Philippians 2:11: 'Christians were in danger of being misunderstood by Gentiles or attacked by Jews as polytheists and needed to safeguard their monotheistic intentions.'[12] Only a very high Christology could have created the danger of such misunderstanding.

All that we know of early Christian attitudes to Jesus confirms that they regarded him as Lord in the highest possible sense. They saw themselves as his slaves, unconditionally bound by his will. They took their very identity from the fact that it was his name they invoked in worship (1 Cor. 1:2). They sang their psalms, hymns and spiritual songs specifically to him (Eph. 5:19). They prayed to him (2 Cor. 12:8). They even expected the praises of the world to come to be directed to him (Rev. 1:6; 5:9; 5:12; 7:10; 15:3).

But the affirmation of Christ as *kurios* does not indicate only that the early Christians applied to Christ all the honour due to the God of the Old Testament. The phrase *kurios Iesous* functioned in two directions. If *kurios* signalised great honour for Jesus, so Jesus signalised unforeseen enriching of *kurios*. The wonder was not only the lordship of Jesus but also the Jesus-hood of the Lord. That *Jahweh* would come to save his people was part of the clear vision of the Old Testament (Pss. 98:9; 96:13). But that his coming should be in the form of Jesus was something else. That the Being One should take our nature, share our experiences and bear our

sins was a monumental re-definition of *Jahweh*. No wonder that
the church should 'stand and gaze in wonder':

> Nailed to a tree, the great Creator suffered
> When that dread weight of foulest sin He bore
> Lo! Satan flees! the Lord of glory triumphs!
> Nothing can with this mighty love compare.

References

1. O. Cullmann, *The Christology of the New Testament*, p. 237.
2. R. Bultmann, *The Theology of the New Testament*, Vol. I, p. 124.
3. A.E.J. Rawlinson, *The New Testament Doctrine of the Christ* (London: Longmans, Green & Co., 1929), p. 235.
4. O. Cullmann, *The Christology of the New Testament*, p. 209.
5. C.F.D. Moule, *The Origin of Christology* (Cambridge: Cambridge University Press, 1977), p. 41.
6. G. Vos, *The Self-Disclosure of Jesus* (Nutley, N.J.: Presbyterian and Reformed, New Edition, 1953), p. 128.
7. G. Vos, *op. cit.*, p. 129.
8. O. Cullmann, *The Early Church* (London: SCM Press, 1966), pp. 62, 69.
9. R. Bultmann, *The Theology of the New Testament*, Vol. I, p. 124.
10. C.F.D. Moule, *The Origin of Christology*, p. 42.
11. C.F.D. Moule, *op. cit.*, p. 43.
12. C.F.D. Moule, *op. cit.*, p. 43.

3

THE SON OF MAN

For centuries theologians understood the title *the Son of Man* as simply the counter-poise to *the Son of God*. It pointed to the Lord's human nature as the latter did to his divine. Calvin, for example, writes: 'And this, too, is the reason why he calls himself the Son of Man, that we may not doubt that we have an entrance into heaven in common with him who clothed himself with our flesh, that he might make us partakers of all his blessings.'[1] The emergence (or re-emergence) of proper historico-critical exegesis in the nineteenth century soon showed, however, that this approach was untenable. Far from pointing to a humiliated and lowly state the designation *Son of Man* referred in many contexts to a pre-existent, majestic figure whose suffering was only a prelude to sovereignty over the cosmos and jurisdiction over all mankind. The passing years have generated an enormous amount of literature on the subject, critical, exegetical and theological. *Son of Man* studies is now a specialism in its own right. Indeed, the field reminds one of the computer-industry: each new publication is rapidly rendered obsolete by its successor.

In this study we shall have to make drastic economies, referring to critical problems only so far as they affect our own limited theological enquiry.

Only on the lips of Jesus

The single most striking feature of the title in the New Testament is that it occurs only on the lips of Jesus. There is only one real exception to this: in Acts 7:56 Luke records that the martyr Stephen saw the heavens opened and the Son of Man standing at the right hand of God. There is an apparent exception, too, in Revelation 1:13: 'On turning I saw in the midst of the lampstands one like a son of man.' But this differs in important respects from the title in the Gospels. John's figure is curiously composite. The terms in which he is described are indeed drawn from Daniel 7:9ff., but

they are terms which in the original context referred not to the
Son of Man but to the Ancient of Days. More important, the phrase
in Revelation 1:13 lacks the definite article: a very important detail,
as we shall see. John does not say that he saw the Son of Man but
one *like a* son of man. The figure is undoubtedly Christ. But the
title is not the same.

Apart from these two instances the title is found only on the
lips of Jesus. As such, however, it occurs frequently. It occurs in
all the Synoptics. It occurs in all the sources behind them. And it
occurs thirteen times in the Gospel of John. What is the significance
of this remarkable distribution?

For one thing, it indicates very clearly that the title *the Son of
Man* was not prevalent in the early church. We do not find it in
the epistles, nor in liturgical fragments, nor in the historical books
(Acts), nor even in the narrative portions of the Gospels themselves.
This makes it virtually certain that the use of the title goes back to
Jesus himself. Why would the early Christians place on his lips a
title they never used themselves? In fact, all the evidence we have
suggests that the trend in the early church was away from the title
the Son of Man. One clear hint of this is that in the case of six of
the Son of Man sayings in the Synoptics the title is replaced by
something else in the parallel passages. For example, the title *Son
of Man* in Matthew 16:13 is replaced by 'I' in the parallel passages
Mark 8:27 and Luke 9:18; *the Son of Man* of Mark 8:31 and Luke
9:22 is replaced by 'him' in Matthew 16:21; and *the Son of Man*
in Matthew 16:28 is replaced by 'kingdom' in Mark 9:1 and Luke
9:27. David R. Jackson has examined these and similar sayings in
an important article in *The Westminster Theological Journal*[2] and
concluded that the external evidence 'gives decisive weight to the
probability that the forms with *the Son of Man* title are prior,
requiring us to view the other forms as interpretative paraphrases'.
By 'external evidence' Jackson means three things: first, the fact
that whereas in later Christian documents (both canonical and non-
canonical) the titles *Lord, Christ* and *Son of God* are popular, the
title *Son of Man* is not; secondly, the tendency to omit the title
even when alluding to a Son of Man saying from the Gospels; thirdly,
the absence of any instance of another title (e.g. *Lord, Christ,*

Jesus) being altered to read *Son of Man*. The traffic was all one-way: towards replacing the Son of Man title with something else.

All this surely rules out the possibility that the Son of Man sayings reflect the church's post-Easter faith and the emergence of a Son of Man Christology. What we have instead is the demise of the Son of Man Christology (peculiar to the Lord himself), and the persistence of the title can be attributed only to the faithfulness of the evangelists. Their usage reflects not the life-situation of the early church but that of the earthly ministry. Why the title should have fallen out of use it is not safe to speculate. It was probably due in some measure to the fact that after the resurrection and ascension the natural way to refer to Jesus was as *Lord*. Besides, *the Son of Man* was, as we shall see, a rather cryptic title. When the church moved after Pentecost to a missionary footing, something more explicit was called for. A gospel which said, 'Jesus is Lord!' was much more natural than one which said, 'Jesus is Son of Man!'

Under the conditions of the earthly ministry, however, *the Son of Man* was the preferred self-designation of Jesus, at least as portrayed by the Synoptics. It is interesting, for example, that when Peter at Caesarea Philippi confesses, 'You are the Christ!' Jesus in his response changes this to *the Son of Man*: 'the Son of Man must suffer many things' (Mark 8:31).

A self-dsignation
But *was* the title a self-designation? Did the evangelists misunderstand the phrase? As has been pointed out by many scholars, the Aramaic term *bar enash* is generic: 'The basic nuance is therefore a human being, corresponding with Greek *anthropos* and Latin *homo*, rather than an individual person.'[3] P.M. Casey writes to similar effect: 'The Aramaic *barnash(a)* is generally agreed to have been a normal term for "man".' Consequently, 'sentences containing *barnash(a)* would not have sufficient referring power to denote a single individual unless the situational and literary context contained features which made this clear.'[4]

The generic reference cannot be rejected out of hand. A prevailing Aramaic idiom is not something to be lightly dismissed!

Besides, the generic use appears clearly in Scripture itself. In Psalm
8:4, for example, *the son of man* is clearly parallel to *man*. It is
also possible that in some of the Son of Man sayings in the Gospels
there is a stress on the Lord's generic humanity. This is particularly
true of John 5:27: God gave him 'authority to execute judgement
because he is Son of Man' (compare Acts 17:31: 'God will judge
the world by *that man* whom he has appointed'). It may even be
true that it was the generic allusion of the phrase which made it
attractive, because it gave it an ambiguity which suited the Lord's
purpose (although, as we shall see, the connection between the
title *the Son of Man* and the Messianic Secret has probably been
over-stressed).

Neither Lindars nor Casey, however, seems prepared to argue
that the phrase as used by Jesus is simply and outrightly generic.
Each appears to want an interpretation which is both self-referring
and generic. There is, however, a difference of emphasis.
According to Casey, *the Son of Man* means mankind and includes
Christ only as one of the race. Lindars understands the phrase
more narrowly: 'the speaker refers to a class of persons with whom
he identifies himself.'⁵ What is common to both scholars is an
insistence that some generic reference is essential. Those sayings
which lack it are unidiomatic and hence unauthentic and can be
discussed as creations of the early church.

But there are serious difficulties in the claim that the phrase
the Son of Man always has some generic reference.

For one thing, it is frequently replaced in parallel passages by
other titles and pronouns which can refer only to Jesus. We have
already seen what happens in Mark 8:29ff., for example: the Lord
substitutes *the Son of Man* for Peter's *Christ*. In other instances
the title is replaced by *I* (Mark 8:27, Luke 9:18, compared with
Matthew 16:13; Matthew 5:11 compared with Luke 6:22; Luke
22:27 compared with Mark 10:45 and Matthew 20:28; and
Matthew 10:32 compared with Luke 12:8). In one other stance it
is replaced by *him* (Matthew 16:21 compared with Mark 8:31 and
Luke 9:22). So far as the evangelists were concerned, in these
instances at least the term *Son of Man* was an exclusive self-
reference on the part of Christ.

Secondly, there is a large group of passages where the generic meaning is simply impossible (despite Lindars' efforts to prove the contrary).[6] One of these is Matthew 8:20: 'Foxes have holes and the birds of the air have nests, but *bar enasha* has nowhere to lay his head.' It is impossible to believe that the contrast here is between foxes and birds on the one hand and mankind on the other. It is simply not true that man as such has nowhere to lay his head. Nor can we identify any group (for example, the Lord and his disciples) to which the language might apply. The specific incident which called forth the Lord's statement was an offer made by one of the scribes, 'Teacher, I will follow you wherever you go.' The Lord's answer is, in effect, 'I have nowhere to lay my head.'

Matthew 11:16-19 is also interesting in this connection: 'John the Baptist came eating no bread and drinking no wine and you said, "He has a demon". The Son of Man came eating and drinking: and you say, "Behold a glutton and a drunkard, a friend of publicans and sinners".' The comparison is not between John the Baptist and some generic entity but between two specific individuals, John and Jesus. The crowd would have been in no doubt as to the one to whom *the Son of Man* referred. They knew who was the friend of publicans and sinners and they knew who was accused of gluttony and drunkenness (after all, they were the accusers). In fact, there was little need for ambiguity. The Lord was not in this context making any subversive or pretentious claims.

When we turn to Matthew 12:32, the issue is not so clear-cut: 'Whoever blasphemes the Son of Man will be forgiven; but whoever blasphemes the Holy Spirit will not be forgiven, either in this age or in the age to come.' It is not surprising that Lindars should write: 'This is a clear case where the generic use of *bar enasha* is required, for the contrast is between slandering men and blaspheming the Spirit of God.'[7] Even so conservative a scholar as Geerhardus Vos was inclined to this view: 'The possibility must be reckoned with that Jesus may have spoken of man generically, and that through misunderstanding in the process of translation into the Greek the title Son of Man slipped in.'[8] Vos notes the efforts of scholars to explain how Jesus may be blasphemed against in some capacity but not in others and concludes: 'But these are

too unnatural to commend themselves. As soon as for *Son of Man*
the simple "man" is substituted, everything becomes perfectly
clear. Speaking a word against a man may receive pardon, but
speaking against the Holy Spirit, and against the One working
through the Holy Spirit (for these two are inseparable) will not
receive pardon, neither in this world, nor in the world to come.'[9]
Over against this, however, we should note that there are clear
signs in the context (especially in Luke's account) that what is
under discussion is man's attitude to Jesus himself: *the Son of
Man* alternates with the first personal pronoun. The saying about
blasphemy is immediately preceded by the words: 'Every one who
acknowledges me before men, the Son of Man also will
acknowledge before the angels of God; but he who denies me
before men will be denied before the angels of God' (Luke 12:8f.).
It would be very confusing if *the Son of Man* were used
immediately afterwards with a generic meaning.

More important, there are serious theological difficulties in
Vos' interpretation. Is it true that blasphemy against Jesus is never
forgiven? How then are we to understand the case of Paul: 'I
formerly blasphemed and persecuted and insulted him; but I
received mercy because I acted ignorantly, in unbelief'(1 Tim.
1:13)? It is highly likely that some distinction must be drawn
between blasphemy against Jesus (especially the veiled Jesus) and
blasphemy against the Spirit; and the key to that distinction
probably lies in Paul's word *ignorantly*, which throws us back at
once upon the ministry of the Spirit. It is the difference between
the blasphemy of one who has been *enlightened* (Heb. 6:4) and
one who has not. If this is so, then in Matthew 12:32 *the Son of
Man* is not a generic title but one which distinguishes Jesus both
from the Holy Spirit and from men in general.

Mark 2:10f. also deals with the question of forgiveness but
from a different point of view: 'But that you may know that the
Son of Man has authority on earth to forgive sins – he said to the
paralytic – "I say to you, Rise, take up your pallet and go home".'
There may be some stress on the Lord's humanness here: he,
although man, has authority to forgive. Yet this could never lead
to the proposition that man generically (or any group of men) has

such authority. The bystanders' question, 'Who can forgive sins but God only?', is particularly pertinent in view of the critical presuppositions which lie behind the rejection of the phrase *Son of Man* as a title. Jesus, we are told, could not have so used it because it was not current in Judaism at the time. Yet we are now told that he taught that man can forgive sins. Was this taught in Judaism at the time? On the contrary, such a claim would have violated the most basic beliefs of his hearers. They would have found the idea monstrous. In fact the reference of the Son of Man title here is totally specific: Jesus, although a man, has authority, even on earth, to forgive sins. Nor is there any possibility here of a Messianic secret. He, and he alone, has such authority.

In Luke 12:8f. it is difficult to find even a trace of the generic sense: 'Everyone who acknowledges me before men, the Son of Man also will acknowledge before the angels of God.' In the parallel passage in Matthew (10:32f.) the phrase *Son of Man* does not occur at all. The first personal pronoun is used throughout: '*I* also will acknowledge before *my* Father who is in heaven.' Matthew clearly thought that *the Son of Man* equals *Jesus*. But this is apparent even in Luke's account of the saying. The idea of the Son of Man acknowledging those who confess him is set between two others: 'Everyone who acknowledges *me*...he who denies *me*.' There is no room for any reference beyond that to Christ himself. We cannot even call the self-reference 'circumlocutory' as Lindars does.[10] It is explicit and exclusive.

Similarly, the language of the Passion predictions is much too detailed and explicit to refer to any but Christ: 'The Son of Man must suffer many things and be rejected by the elders and the chief priests and the scribes, and be killed, and after three days rise again' (Mark 8:31). As Mark comments, the Lord was speaking 'plainly' (verse 32). The disciples were certainly in no doubt. Peter understood well enough to take him aside and rebuke him; and in the ensuing context, *Son of Man* alternates with *I*: 'whoever is ashamed of me, of him will the Son of Man be ashamed' (Mark 8:38). These remarks apply equally to Mark 10:45: 'Even the Son of Man came not to be served but to serve and to give his life a ransom for many.' Whether *kai* here means *even* or *also* it distinguishes the Son of Man from the generality of men and specifically from the disciples (to whom he is an example, Luke 22:25ff.). Besides, giving one's life as a ransom for the many was not (and is not) a generic human experience. It was specific to Christ himself and by this stage in his ministry he was teaching that explicitly.

We find a similar situation in Luke 22:22 and its parallels: 'The Son of Man goes as it has been determined: but woe to that man by whom he is betrayed.' Even in this Lucan form the allusion to the betrayal by Judas is specific enough. It is even more so in Matthew 26:20ff.: ' "Truly I say to you, one of you will betray me." And they began to say to him one after another, "Lord, is it I?" He answered, "He who has dipped his hand in the dish with me, will betray me. The Son of Man goes...".'

What is true of the Passion sayings is even more true of the Parousia sayings: they are neither generic nor circumlocutory but specific and unambiguous. Mark 8:38 is of particular interest: 'Whoever shall be ashamed of me in this adulterous and sinful generation, of him shall the Son of Man be ashamed when he comes in the glory of his Father with the holy angels.' This is totally unambiguous. The Coming One is *me*, the very Jesus of whom so many have been ashamed. The event itself, too, is utterly non-generic. It is a coming in *glory*, a coming with the *holy angels* and a coming to *judge*. It is noteworthy, too, that in this passage the Son of Man merges with the Son of God: 'the Son of Man is coming in the glory of *his* Father.'

Even more striking is Matthew 26:63-64: 'The High Priest said to him, "I adjure you by the living God, tell us if you are the Christ, the Son of God." Jesus said to him, "You have said so. But I tell you, hereafter you will see the Son of Man seated at the right hand of the Power, and coming on the clouds of heaven...".' Here again is a totally non-generic experience, in fact, two experiences: the enthronement of the Son of Man and the coming of the Son of Man. Here, too, there is an identification (this time even more explicit) of the Son of Man with the Son of God: the question, 'Are you the Son of God?' is answered by saying, 'Yes, I am the Son of Man.' Nor is there any lack of definiteness. Whatever need there had been previously to keep the Messiahship secret there was no need to do so now. Jesus' meaning was only too clear: 'Then the High Priest tore his robes and said, "He has uttered blasphemy! What need of any more witnesses? You have now heard his blasphemy!" '

According to Casey, however, sayings with an exclusive reference to Jesus are unauthentic. Why? Because they do not conform to Aramaic idiom and must therefore be creations of the early church: 'If anything like the theory of Lindars and myself is right, examples of this idiom must have a generic or general level of meaning.'[11] Stated otherwise, those sayings which apply specifically and exclusively to Jesus 'do not permit of satisfactory Aramaic reconstructions'. Applying this criterion, Casey is able to dismiss the predictions of the Parousia as the creations of the early church and to claim that a significant proportion of the Son of Man sayings in the Gospels are unauthentic.

This looks suspiciously like arguing in a circle. The phrase *the Son of Man*, we are told, always has a generic reference; this is countered by saying, But some of the instances we meet in the Gospels clearly do not have such a reference: ah! but these are unauthentic; why? because they do not have a generic reference. We pretend to be framing a theory which suits the facts and end rejecting facts which do not suit our theory. How precarious the whole argument is becomes even more obvious when we recall how doubtful the generic reference is in those passages which Casey and Lindars accept as authentic. In fact, by their criterion there is probably not a single authentic Son of Man saying in the Gospels.

But there are other difficulties, too, in Casey's argument. As Morna D. Hooker points out: 'It is questionable whether the early church was quite so ready to put Christological terms into the mouth of Jesus as is supposed.'[12] If the early church was so 'creative', why, for example, does the Jesus of the Gospels not refer to himself more often as 'the Christ'? The evidence we have already seen as to the way that the Son of Man passages were treated in parallel passages, in the epistles and in post-biblical literature shows very clearly that the trend in the early church was

not to create new Son of Man sayings but to replace existing ones
with some other title.

It is also exceedingly difficult on Casey's theory to account
for the peculiar distribution of Son of Man sayings. Why is the
title found only on the lips of Jesus? Why, if the early Christians
were in the business of multiplying Son of Man sayings did they
not insert them in narrative or in address to Jesus (the title occurs
frequently in Ezekiel in the vocative)? Furthermore, why, if they
wanted to create predictions of the Passion, should they choose
the title Son of Man, associated as the phrase was with the ideas
of enthronement and judgement? As free creations of the church
the pattern of the Son of Man sayings is inexplicable.

How important is the fact, insisted on by so many scholars,
that there is no precedent in pre-Christian (or contemporary)
Judaism for the use of the Son of Man as a title? Current studies
seem to be facing both ways on this issue. The passion and parousia
sayings are dismissed because 'all of them have an excellent *sitz
im leben* in the known concerns of the early church';[13] sayings in
which the Son of Man has an exclusive self-reference (that is, it
functions as a title) are dismissed because they have *no* context in
the life of the early church. Which is it to be? Is conformity to the
first-century context of meaning to be deemed a plus or a minus
for the sayings recorded in the Gospels? In the current instance it
is surely safest to conclude that if the title was not current in
Judaism the early church had little incentive to invent it and
therefore its presence in the Gospels reflects only faithfulness to
the original language of Jesus.

Some time, however, we must ask just how certain we can be
that the title *Son of Man* does not occur in Judaism. It is to be
found, for example, in *The Similitudes of Enoch*, but this work is
confidently dated towards the end of the first century and cannot
be taken as evidence of pre-Christian usage. On the other hand, is
it likely that the titular use of the Son of Man suddenly appeared
from nowhere? It seems reasonable to suppose that behind *The
Similitudes* there lies oral tradition antedating (maybe by a
considerable period) the actual date of composition. It would have
been strange, too, had such a titular use grown up in Judaism *after*

the emergence of Christianity. The occurrence of the title in the upstart new religion would have been a strong disincentive to its adoption by traditionalists.

Mistranslated

The position taken by Casey, Lindars and such older scholars as T.W. Manson also requires us to believe that the evangelists mistranslated the original Aramaic phrase, *bar enash*. Had they known as much Aramaic as modern scholars they would have understood the phrase simply as equivalent to *ho anthropos*! Instead, and with perverse consistency (there is not a single instance of *the Son of Man* being replaced by *man* in a parallel text) they render it *ho huios tou anthropou*, which, according to Lindars, means 'the man's son': 'It thus appears,' he writes,[14] 'that, in the Greek *ho huios tou anthropou*, we have a much too literal translation of the Aramaic.' It was this mistake which made possible the use of the Son of Man as a title: 'This usage is a peculiarity of secondary developments in the sayings tradition, which became possible only because the Greek translation of the Aramaic sayings turned the idiomatic *bar enasha* into an exclusive self-reference.'[15] T.W. Manson wrote to the same effect: 'The translator of an Aramaic record of the teaching of Jesus might misunderstand the word in any given case. The evangelist compiling his Gospel from sources oral or written might equally make mistakes.'[16]

. One cannot but feel uneasy, however, about assuming as a matter of course that the evangelists could be mistaken about something as elementary as this. They were as fluent in Aramaic as Jesus himself and some of them (Luke in particular) were completely at home in Greek. They were no more likely to miss the idiomatic meaning of *bar enash(a)* than I am to give a literal translation of the Gaelic, '*C'ail thu cur d'aghaidh an nochd?*' (literally, 'Where are you putting your face tonight?'; actually, 'Where are you going?'). The idea that twentieth-century scholars can detect the subtle nuances of Jesus' vocabulary better than his contemporaries (not to mention his apostles) is not one that on the face of things has much to commend it. The caution uttered by

C.S. Lewis needs to be taken seriously: 'The idea that a man or writer should be opaque to those who lived in the same culture, spoke the same language, shared the same habitual imagery and unconscious assumptions, and yet be transparent to those who have none of those advantages, is in my opinion preposterous. There is an *a priori* improbability in it which almost no argument and no evidence could counterbalance.'[17]

Definite article

C.F.D. Moule[18] lays great stress on the fact that in the sayings of Jesus the title Son of Man always has the definite article: 'The phrase is not, in fact, "Son of Man" but "*the* Son of Man", with the definite article.' The only exception is John 5:27: 'The Father has given him authority to execute judgement because he is (a) Son of Man.' Even here, however, the phrase may in effect be definite, the omission of the article being idiomatic. In Acts 7:56 (Stephen's words, 'I see the heaven opened, and the Son of Man standing at the right hand of God') the phrase still has the article. But in every other instance of its use by someone other than Jesus it is anarthrous (Heb. 2:6; Rev. 1:13; 14:14). What is even more remarkable, Moule can write: 'There is to the best of my knowledge only one instance in Hebrew literature before the New Testament of the definite article used with the singular, "*The* Son of Man".' Even this one instance is probably an afterthought. The Lord's usage is unique.

But what is the significance of the article? According to Moule it is demonstrative. Jesus is not simply *a* son of man. He is *that* Son of Man: a particular one. The question is, Which? Moule is in no doubt: 'This phrase was demonstrative because it expressly referred to Daniel's "Son of Man".'

Two considerations favour Moule's view.

First, this is precisely the force of the definite article in the Ethiopic version of *The Similitudes of Enoch*. The first allusion to Daniel's Son of Man in this work is at 46:1. Here it lacks the article: 'And with him (that is, the Ancient of Days) was another whose countenance was like a son of man.' All the subsequent references to this figure are definite and demonstrative. Enoch at once asks concerning *that* Son of Man and in such a context any self-referring use of the title would be tantamount to saying, 'I am *that* Son of Man.'

More important, in several of the Son of Man sayings the allusion to Daniel is unmistakeable. This is true, for example, in Matthew 24:30: 'They will see the Son of Man coming on the clouds of heaven with power and great glory.' We find the same thing in Matthew 26:64: 'Hereafter you will see the Son of Man seated at the right hand of the Power, and coming on the clouds of heaven.' Judging by these statements it is undeniable that Jesus saw himself very clearly in terms of the Danielic Son of Man. This is a conclusion with which in principle Lindars agrees, although his overall position differs substantially from Moule's: 'In so far as the Son of Man is used as a title in the sayings tradition, it carried with it the identification with the Danielic figure.... From this point of view the definite article in the Greek form used in the Gospel sayings has the force of a demonstrative. But it is important to remember that this applies only when there are Danielic allusions in the context.'[19]

Yet we cannot make a simple transference of the details of Daniel 7:9ff. to the New Testament Son of Man. Certainly there is significant overlap. But there are also curious differences between the two pictures. For example, in the New Testament sayings it is the Son of Man who judges. This is clearly implied, for example, in Mark 8:38: 'Whoever shall be ashamed of me in this adulterous and sinful generation, of him also shall the Son of Man be ashamed when he comes in the glory of his Father with the holy angels.' The same idea is explicit in John 5:27: 'The Father has given him authority to execute judgement because he is (the) Son of Man.' In Daniel, however, judgement is executed by the Ancient of Days: 'Thrones were placed and one that was ancient of days took his seat.' Judgement was given *for* the Son of Man and those he represents, 'the saints of the Most High' (Dan. 7:14-22). In Revelation 1:13ff. we find an even more extraordinary divergence from Daniel. The risen Lord appears as 'one like a son of man' and the allusions to the Danielic context are unmistakeable, but the details of the ensuing description correspond to Daniel's

Ancient of Days, not to his Son of Man: 'his head and his hair were white as wool, white as snow; his eyes were like a flame of fire, his feet were like burnished bronze, refined as in a furnace' (Rev. 1:14-15f.; cf. Dan. 7:9f.). Over and above these differences in detail, of course, the emphasis on humiliation and suffering, so prominent in many of the Gospel Son of Man sayings, is totally absent from Daniel.

It is clear, therefore, that we cannot make the Danielic vision the measure of the significance of the Son of Man as the Lord's preferred self-designation. Far less can we make any prevailing interpretations of Daniel a limiting factor in our interpretation. The Lord was not saying, 'I am the very Son of Man you are expecting.' Instead, in taking the title to himself, the Lord modified it profoundly, bringing in an emphasis on suffering and an emphasis on judgement which were no part of the original, Danielic portrait.

Why then *the* Son of Man? Why *that* Son of Man? Why did he describe himself in Danielic terms at all? The most likely answer is the one offered by Vos (who is very conscious of the differences between the situation in Daniel and the sayings recorded in the Gospels): 'The main thing these passages have derived from Daniel is the atmosphere of the supernatural in which they are steeped.'[20] The Lord's use of the title is not a *claim*: a claim would presuppose that the title was prevalent among his hearers and that its meaning was plain. Neither of these conditions can be met. The title reflects the Lord's self-understanding. That self-understanding is one of modified messiahship. More important, it is one pervaded by the other-worldly, the uncanny and the invincible. His realm is that of the Ancient of Days; his status-symbol, the clouds of heaven; his jurisdiction, universal; his dominion, everlasting; his destiny, glory and sovereignty; the proper response to him, worship.

There is much here that fits in well with the classic emphases of Chalcedon, according to which the Lord was not a human being destined for exaltation (or even for deification) but a divine being who has taken human nature and human consciousness. When that human consciousness thinks of his self and of his home and of his primal relationships, it thinks not in earthly terms (of the home in Nazareth and of Mary and Joseph) but of heaven and of the Ancient of Days, because it is from these (if Chalcedon is right) that he takes his identity. What the Son of Man sayings are telling us is this: as his human mind pored over the Old Testament he found self-understanding pre-eminently in Daniel's Son of Man. There were very, very few allusions in the earlier revelation to the divine fatherhood and sonship: too few to give him any light. He would have found some light, no doubt, in the allusions to the Messiah, some too in the Son of David and some sombre insights in the portrait of the Suffering Servant. But the Son of Man described most fully who he was and what he was destined for. It was free from the compromising associations of other Messianic titles (just as, in another connection, *agape* was free from the associations of *eros*). It expressed simultaneously a special relationship with God and a special relationship with man. It orientated him towards the heaven from which he had come and towards which he was moving. It reminded him that the sufferings which were his lot would have glory as their sequel. But that glory would not simply be man's glory. It would be the Son of Man's, and synonymous with that of the Ancient of Days. He would enjoy it not simply as a man, but as *the* Man, in whom would be fulfilled the promise of Psalm 8:4 and more fundamentally of Genesis 1:28. Never for a moment could he forget that he was Servant. But he was a Servant who would be exalted and be very high (Isa. 52:13).

Three categories

As has often been pointed out, the Son of Man sayings fall into three categories: those referring to the Lord's earthly life and circumstances; those referring to his Passion; and those referring to the Parousia. The subject-matter of the sayings is obviously wide-ranging. But despite the variations in perspective there emerges a clear and coherent picture of the figure to whom the title refers.

First, he is pre-existent. This is suggested in Mark 10:45: 'Even the Son of Man came not to be served but to serve, and to give his life a ransom for many.' Jesus' presence in the world and his role as servant are the result of a deliberate intention formed before he came. But the idea of pre-existence is particularly prominent in some of the Johannine Son of Man sayings. In John 3:13, for example, we read: 'No one has ascended into heaven except the one who descended from heaven, even the Son of Man' (some manuscripts add, "who is in heaven"). Similar language occurs in John 6:62: 'What if you were to see the Son of Man ascending where he was before?' Such passages portray very clearly a Christ who saw his time on earth as only an interlude. His existence did not begin with the Advent. Nor will it end with his death. The incarnation represents Christ temporarily pitching his tent among men (John 1:14).

Secondly, the current weakness, poverty and servility of the Son of Man are really quite remarkable. This is the point of many of the sayings which refer to the earthly life. As Geerhardus Vos points out, 'The thought of humiliation and death is not analytically obtained from the name Son of Man. Rather, it is joined to it on the principle of contrast. It is not that He must undergo humiliation, suffering and death *because* He is the Son of Man, but that *although* He is the Son of Man such a destiny is, paradoxically, in store for Him.'[21] One of the clearest examples of this is the saying recorded in Luke 9:58: 'Foxes have holes, and birds of the air have nests; but the Son of Man has nowhere to lay his head.' The generic interpretation, as we have seen, is impossible here. Vos is surely right again: 'The very point of the saying obviously is that the highest of the high, according to the name borne by Him, should nevertheless have to do without such common creature comforts as even foxes and birds enjoy.'[22] It is remarkable that he (*he*, of all men) should have nowhere to lay his head. There is a hint to the same effect in Mark 10:45: '*even* the Son of Man came not to be served but to serve.' Compare this with John 13:14: 'If I, then, your Lord and Teacher, have washed your feet, you also ought to wash one another's feet.' The Son of Man of Mark 10:45 carries the same moral authority as the Lord and Teacher of John 13:14. The fact that *he* should wash men's feet (or suffer) is remarkable even to the point of being offensive. This is underlined by Peter's reaction in Mark 8:32 and John 13:8. In the former passage he rebukes Christ. In the latter he says, 'You will never wash my feet!'

Thirdly, the suffering of the Son of Man has redemptive significance. The fact that he would suffer came like a bombshell to the disciples at Caesarea Philippi: 'The Son of Man must suffer many things and be rejected by the elders and the chief priests and the scribes and be killed and after three days rise again' (Mark 8:31). The *must* was not the *must* of circumstances or of the social and political inevitability of such a person provoking the resentment of the authorities. It was, first of all, the *must* of his own intention: he had come precisely in order to suffer. But it was also the *must* of the Father's command: 'This commandment have I received from my Father' (John 10:18). In Gethsemane, the Lord sees precisely how inescapable the suffering is. It is impossible for the cup to pass (Mark 14:36). The reason for that suffering is clearly indicated in Mark 10:45: 'The Son of Man came to give his life a ransom for many.' In this saying, the Lord effects a remarkable synthesis between the Son of Man perspective and the Suffering Servant perspective. In Isaiah 53:12, it is the Servant who pours out his life, bears the iniquities of the many and makes his soul an offering for sin. There is no hint of any of this in Daniel's vision. The Son of Man is a glorious and triumphant figure. But Jesus brings the two strands together: The Son of Man is to be bruised and put to grief. Why? His suffering is not arbitrary, nor is it a mere martyrdom; nor is it only the result of his solidarity with his people. It is redemptive. It justifies the many and secures their peace (Isa. 53:5, 11). How? As a sin-offering (verse 10), effective through vicarious suffering (Isa. 53:5). He bore sin. But it was not his own sin. It was the sin of the many. It was our sin: he was wounded for *our* transgressions and bruised for *our* iniquities.

In such an understanding Daniel has, at least on the face of things, been left far behind. Yet, it is the glory of the Danielic figure that creates the problem to which the doctrine of the atonement is the answer. It is difficult enough to understand how the Son of Man can have nowhere to lay his head. But what are we to make of his being crucified? The doctrine of vicarious atonement is not without its own difficulties. But without it, Calvary (and the whole Christ-event) is a shambles. On the other hand, if the glory of the victim creates a paradox which demands resolution, the magnificence of what the cross achieved is itself an element to be fed back into our understanding of the Person. That the death should have such unique significance surely points to something startling in him whose death it is. He is not just a man, but *the* Man: even the Last Man. The mystery of his Person lies beneath the mystery of the atonement. It is as himself that he is the propitiation (1 John 2:2).

Fourthly, the Son of Man will one day be vindicated and glorified. This is the special emphasis of the Parousia sayings, but it is by no means confined to them. It occurs, for example, in the prediction of the Passion recorded in Mark 8:31: 'The Son of Man must suffer many things, and be rejected by the elders, and the chief priests and the scribes, and be killed: and after three days rise again.' The exaltation is also the theme of the only Son of Man saying recorded outwith the Gospels, the words of Stephen in Acts 7:56: 'Behold, I see the heavens opened, and the Son of Man standing on the right hand of God.' This emphasis clearly reflects Daniel 7:13ff., but it is by no means alien to the Servant Songs of Isaiah. We must not forget that the very song which speaks most of the suffering is headed by the affirmation, 'My servant shall be exalted and extolled and be very high' and ends with the promise that one day 'he will divide the spoil with the strong' (Isa. 52:13; 53:12).

The exaltation itself includes several different elements. Mark 8:31, for example, speaks only of resurrection: 'after three days he will rise again.' In Acts 7:56 the Son of Man is seen standing at the right hand of God. Maybe it is slightly ironic that what points technically to the heavenly *session* of Christ should speak of him as *standing*. In the Johannine sayings, the particular emphasis, so far as the exaltation is concerned, falls on two points: his return to his former position and his role as judge. The former is referred to in John 6:62, 'What if you were to see the Son of Man ascending where he was before?' (to the glory he had with the Father before the world was, John 17:5); the latter is referred to in John 5:22, 27, 'The Father has committed all judgement to the Son because he is (the) Son of Man.'

But there is no doubt that it is the Parousia sayings which speak most clearly of the exaltation. The sayings themselves contain several remarkable features. For example, in some of them the title *Son of Man* is fused with *the Son of God*. One instance of this is Mark 8:38, where the phrase 'the glory of his Father' clearly postulates God as Father of the Son of Man. The same thing occurs in Mark 14:62: 'You shall see the Son of Man sitting on the right hand of the Power and coming in the clouds of heaven.' The intriguing thing here is that the words are a response to the question, 'Are you the Christ, the Son of the Blessed?' The Lord replies by saying, virtually, 'Yes! I am the Son of Man!', which strongly suggests that instinctively, if not also conceptually, he saw the titles *Son of Man* and *Son of God* as convertible.

Another striking feature of the Parousia sayings is their emphasis on what we may call the insignia of majesty. The most obvious of these is 'the clouds of heaven' (Mark 13:26; 14:62), a direct allusion to Daniel 7:13. As we have seen, clouds are frequently associated with *Jahweh* in the Old Testament: 'Ascribe ye strength unto God; his excellency is over Israel, and his strength is in the clouds' (Ps. 68:34). Sometimes the cloud (or clouds) had theophanic import. They gave visibility to the presence of God. During the Wilderness Journey, for example, the people of God were led by a Pillar of Cloud (Num. 9:15ff.). When God appeared on Mount Sinai (Exod. 19:16) 'there were thunders and lightnings and a thick cloud upon the mountain'; and on the Mount of Transfiguration, the voice of the Father spoke from a bright cloud (Matt. 17:5). The clouds which accompany the Parousia belong to the same symbolism. They are tokens of the supernatural and attestations of the divine activity and presence. Nor are they alone. The returning Saviour is also accompanied by angels and surrounded in some visible way by the glory of his Father. In these respects, the Parousia is a reversal of the *kenosis*. At the First Advent, men saw what looked like a man, and no more. Whatever glory he possessed was obscured. He came *incognito*. At the Second Advent, the glory will be fully unveiled and the majesty will be unmistakeable. The Parousia will be an unqualified *apokalupsis* and *epiphany*.

The Parousia sayings also bring out very clearly the supremacy of Christ. One day, men will see him sitting at the right hand of the Power (Mark 14:62) and standing at the right hand of God (Acts 7:56). For the One who once was made a curse, the wheel will come full circle. He will occupy a position of favour and authority. In Revelation 1:13, one like a son of man stands amid the lampstands, proclaiming himself the First and the Last, supreme even over Death and Hades. The Danielic flavour of the whole passage is unmistakeable. The same is probably true of Matthew 28:18: 'All authority is mine in heaven and on earth.' 'When our Lord uttered these words,' writes E.J. Young, 'There can be no doubt but that He had in mind this passage in Daniel.'[23] Like that of the Danielic figure, the empire of the New Testament Son of Man is universal, eternal and all-conquering. It is for this reason that our attitude to him is so decisive. 'Whoever is ashamed of me and of my words of him will the Son of Man be ashamed when he comes in the glory of his Father' (Mark 8:38).

But it is impossible to stop here. The supremacy points beyond itself to the fact that the Son of Man is divine. The functions involved in the supremacy demand this. Who but God can function as universal, eternal and unchallengeable Sovereign and Judge? But the sayings themselves contain many details which point in the same direction and save us from the need to rely on inference. In John 3:13, for example, it is explicitly said that he is of heavenly origin: 'No one has ascended into heaven, save he that descended from heaven, even the Son of Man.' The same fact is indicated in the allusion to the clouds. To come in or with the clouds of heaven is to come from heaven. The Parousia is a Theophany. And as we have seen, there is clearly a fluidity between the Son of Man and the Son of God. The one title merges easily into the other. Even the sayings which refer to the earthly life of the Lord often presuppose his deity. For example, he claims authority, even on earth, to forgive sins: something which the Jewish onlookers rightly see as a divine prerogative (Mark 2:7). In the same way he claims to be Lord of the Sabbath, that day which *Jahweh* claimed specifically as his own: 'If you turn back your foot from doing your pleasure on my holy day, and call the sabbath a delight, and the holy day of the LORD honourable, then I will feed you with the heritage of Jacob your father' (Isa. 58:13f.). The Son of Man is Lord of *this* Sabbath. God's day is *his* day, and it is up to him to decide what behaviour befits it. It is thoroughly in line with this that the Son of Man should command unhesitating and unconditional allegiance. Whoever rejects or disowns the Son of Man, his doom is sealed. In the very context (Luke 9:57ff.) where Jesus remarks that the Son of Man has nowhere to lay his head, there are two other sayings which bring out very powerfully his assumptions as to his own authority. One occurs in verse 60: 'Let the dead bury the dead (even though it be your own father); you go and proclaim the kingdom of God.' The other is in verse 62: 'No one who puts his hand to the plough and looks back is fit for the kingdom of God.' Obligations to the Son of Man take precedence over everything else in life; and commitment to him must be irreversible. These assumptions as to his own standing come to a head in the saying recorded in Mark 14:21: 'The Son of Man goes as it is written of him. But woe to that man by whom the Son of Man is betrayed! It would have been better for that man if he had never been born.'

The older theology, as we have seen, regarded the titles *Son of Man* and *Son of God* as pointing respectively to his human and divine natures. But this clearly fails to do justice to the pattern we find in the New Testament. There it points to the whole Christ and is indeed the Saviour's preferred self-designation. As such it both connotes and denotes a Being who is pre-existent, heavenly and divine. Yet it would be premature to dismiss completely the idea that the use of the title is related in some way to the fact that the Lord participated in human nature. *Bar enash* does mean, after all, *a man*; the figure in Daniel 7:13 is 'like a man'; and the figure in Revelation 1:13 is also 'like a man'. As we have already seen, the role given to Christ in judgement is related to the fact that he is a man (John 5:27; Acts 17:31). Furthermore, the New Testament clearly emphasises the part played by *a man* in redemption, particularly in contrasting the man Adam and the man Jesus. In Romans 5:15, for example, Paul writes, 'If the many died through one man's trespass, much more have the grace of God and the

gracious gift of the one man Jesus Christ abounded for the
advantage of the many.' The same perspective appears in two
passages in First Corinthians. In 1 Corinthians 15:21 we read: 'For
as by a man came death, by a man has come also the resurrection
of the dead'; while 1 Corinthians 15:45 tells us: 'The first man
Adam became a living being; the last Adam became a life-giving
Spirit.' Such passages are particularly interesting in view of current
tendencies to internalise the atonement, as if it were something
that took place supra-temporally within the life of the Godhead
itself. However true it is that Christ, both as Priest and as Sacrifice,
is *homoousios* with the Father we must not ignore the stress laid
on Christ's humanity. God indeed provides the sacrifice and even
becomes the sacrifice. Yet he does it from man's side and even
from within humanity. The Reconciler is not only the Son of God
but the Last Adam, covering by his obedience the disobedience
of the First. Sin is borne not only in the heart of the Godhead but
in Christ's body on the tree (1 Pet. 2:24). It is condemned in the
flesh of Jesus Christ (Rom. 8:3). From this point of view, the
manhood of Christ, rooting his work firmly in the world of the
seen and the temporal, is essential to the atonement.

But probably our most interesting perspective on the manhood
of the Son of Man is in Hebrews 2:5ff.: 'For he has not subjected
to angels the coming world-order, of which we are speaking. But
one testified somewhere, What is man, that you remember him?
or the son of man, that you care for him?' The writer goes on
(verse 9) to identify Christ as the One in whom this promise is
fulfilled. He is the Son of Man who, for a little, becomes lower
than the angels, but eventually is crowned with glory and honour.
The background to the whole passage, however, is not Daniel
7:13ff., but Psalm 8:3-8; and behind the Psalm itself there is the
language of Genesis 1:28: 'Be fruitful and multiply, and fill the
earth and subdue it; and have dominion over the fish of the sea
and over the birds of the air and over every living thing that moves
upon the earth.' Christ is the One in whom the so-called Cultural
Mandate finds its fulfilment. He inherits and dominates the coming
world-order (we cannot discount the possibility that the subjugating
will be a long-term process, as it was to be for pre-Fall Man). This

is not true, however, in some exclusive sense, as if he *alone* enjoyed the dominion. Just as Adam's seed would have participated in Adam's supremacy so the Son of Man's seed will participate in his triumph. Having brought many sons to glory (Heb. 2:10) he can survey his domain and say, 'Here am I and the children God has given me' (Heb. 2:13). The picture is the same as we have in Revelation 20:4, where the saints reign with Christ; or Romans 8:29, which portrays Christ as the first-born among many brethren and even suggests that the creation of a worshipping community is the motive which underlies God's eternal predestination.

A corporate figure

But what is the precise relation between the Son of Man and mankind and particularly between him and the people of God? Is the Son of Man a corporate figure? As long ago as 1931 T.W. Manson argued that in Daniel 'the phrase is not to be understood literally but as an ideogram, if one may so describe it, meaning "the people of the saints of the Most High".'[24] Manson extended this theory to the Gospels where, as he saw it, the Son of Man was an embodiment of the Remnant Idea or 'the manifestation of the Kingdom of God on earth in a people wholly devoted to their heavenly king'.[25] C.F.D. Moule expressed general sympathy with Manson's idea: the Son of Man was 'a symbol of the martyr-group of loyal Jews coming through persecution and vindicated by God'.[26] Morna D. Hooker followed the same line: 'The righteous in Israel are the true Son of Man.'[27] Moule reiterated his position in a later work: 'The human figure of Daniel 7 stands not for some angelic host but for God's loyal people vindicated in the court of heaven after tribulation.'[28]

But there are fatal objections to any straightforward identification of the Son of Man with the people of God. For one thing, it does not fit the picture we have in Daniel itself. For example: In what sense do the saints come in the clouds of heaven? Surely their approach to the throne is upwards (from earth), not downwards (from heaven)? Furthermore, what, on Manson's interpretation, are we to make of Daniel 7:14? If 'all peoples, nations and languages' are to serve the Son of Man, are the Saints of the Most High excepted? The query is especially important in view of the fact that in Revelation 7:9 these saints are described in terms which are distinctly reminiscent of Daniel 7:14: 'I looked, and behold a great multitude, which no man could number, of all nations, and kindreds and peoples and tongues, stood before the throne and before the Lamb.' It is worth noting, too, that the verb rendered *serve (pilach)* appears to mean something more than political service, something, indeed, close to religious worship. Outside Daniel 7, it occurs only in Daniel 3: and there it refers to the worship offered to the image set up by Nebuchadnezzar. Verse 28 is typical: Shadrach, Meshach and Abednego 'yielded up their bodies rather than *serve* and worship any God except their own God'. Nowhere in the Scripture is there any hint that worship may be offered to the people of God. Conversely, their own relation to the Messiah is precisely that they serve him.

But even if the corporate interpretation could be harmonised with the details of Daniel 7:13ff., there are crucial differences between the Old Testament vision and its New Testament development. One of these concerns the allusion in Revelation 1:13: 'I saw in the midst of the lampstands one like a son of man.' As we have seen, the details of the ensuing description are taken not from Daniel's description of the Son of Man but from his description of the Ancient of Days. This is perfectly understandable if the Son of Man is a close associate of the Ancient of Days. John's description reflects a legitimate communication of attributes. It is much more difficult to explain (and to justify) if the Son of Man is identical with the saints.

More important, in the transition from the Old Testament to the New there is, as we have also seen, a reversal of roles in connection with judgement. In Daniel, judgement is given in favour of the Son of Man: in the Gospels, judgement is executed *by* the Son of Man. This presents no problem if the Son of Man is the Messiah. But it creates real difficulties if the Son of Man is identical with the people of God. It is true, of course, that the New Testament does ascribe some role in the Judgement to the saints and especially to the apostles: 'Do you not know that the saints will judge the world?' asks Paul (1 Cor. 6:2). 'In the regeneration, when the Son of Man will sit on the throne of his glory, you who have followed me shall also sit on twelve thrones, judging the twelve tribes of Israel,' says Christ in Matthew 19:28. But in this latter passage, whatever the role of the people of God, they are clearly distinguished from the Son of Man himself. He is the One who sits on the Throne of Glory, exercising judgement in God's name. This, surely, is the overriding emphasis in biblical allusions to what Wesley called 'The Great Assize'. Furthermore, the world judged by Christ clearly includes 'the saints of the Most High': '*We* must all appear before the judgement-seat of Christ' (2 Cor. 5:10). This is expressed with special solemnity in Revelation 20:12: 'And I saw the dead, small and great, stand before God; and the books were opened; and another book was opened, which is the book of life: and the dead were judged out of those things which were written in the books, according to their works.' These words make clear that the judgement is universal, extending even to those whose names are written in the Book of Life. Any judgement exercised *by* the saints can only be an adjunct to this, and subordinate to it.

When we turn to the Son of Man sayings as actually recorded in the Gospels it soon becomes clear that the corporate interpretation simply will not fit them. Manson's own caution is worth recalling here: the interpretation must stand or fall 'as it furnishes or fails to furnish a satisfying explanation of the Gospels'.[29] But far from explaining the Gospels, the corporate interpretation makes them nonsense. This becomes clear the moment we substitute 'the saints of the Most High' for 'the Son of Man' in the most familiar sayings. Are the saints of the Most High lords of the Sabbath? Have they nowhere to lay their heads? Have they authority to forgive sins? Must they be killed and after three days rise again? Will they come in great power and glory? Do they give their lives for the redemption of mankind? Is it critical for men's destiny that they be not ashamed of them?

Manson himself is conscious of the difficulty and reacts by questioning the authenticity of such sayings: some are rejected on textual grounds, others dismissed as editorial revisions, yet others as mistranslations ('son of man' for 'man') and others again relegated to apocalyptic symbols.

It is difficult to have any confidence in such procedure. If we begin with the assumption that our interpretation must fit the Gospel sayings it will hardly do to say, Yes they do, in a fraction of the instances, and the remainder are unauthentic. As has been argued above, the evangelists were better placed to translate Aramaic than modern scholars (if only because they were present themselves on the occasions they record and were able to observe the whole semantic context, including such things as body-language, tone of voice, emphasis and audience-needs and reaction). We have also seen that the tendency within the New Testament was not at all towards creating new Son of Man sayings but towards replacing the title with something else in sayings where it already existed. The truth is that in the vast majority of existing Son of Man sayings the meaning 'the saints of the Most High' would be utterly incongruous and we cannot allow the difficulty to be eliminated by a critical conjuring-trick.

When Manson begins to work out the implications of his position he gets into very troubled theological waters. This is particularly true of his remarks on the fellowship in suffering between Christ and his people. Manson argues that as Christ saw things his people (the Remnant) were to share his destiny, including his sufferings. Their sacrifice, with his, was to be the price of the world's redemption: 'What was in the mind of Jesus was that he and his followers *together* should share that destiny which he describes as the Passion of the Son of Man: that he and they *together* should be the Son of Man, the Remnant that saves by service and self-sacrifice, the organ of God's redemptive purpose in the world.'[33] He even goes on to say: 'There is not a hint that he would not have allowed them to go to the cross with him, had their courage not failed. The evidence is all the other way.' In support of this construction Manson draws on such Pauline passages as Colossians 1:24, where the apostle speaks of his own sufferings as supplying what is lacking in the sufferings of Christ.

All this is highly plausible and some of it even deeply moving. But on closer examination it bristles with difficulties. The Remnant, we are told, *saves* by service and self-sacrifice. But who saves the Remnant? Surely Christ's suffering *for* them goes before their suffering *with* him: just as in Paul's case any suffering of his is only a sequel to the staggering fact that 'the Son of God loved *me* and gave himself for *me*'? Again: how are we to relate the suffering of the Remnant to the action of God the Father, upon which the New Testament lays such stress in connection with the work of salvation? Could we ever say that God so loved the world that he gave the saints of the Most High so that those who believe in them should never perish but should have everlasting life? Yet again: surely, in the last analysis, the very point of the atonement is that the saints of the Most High do *not* suffer, or at least do not suffer what Christ suffered? The sin-bearing is localised, limited and concentrated in Christ. God condemns sin in *his* flesh, with the result that there is absolutely *no* condemnation to those who are in Christ Jesus (Rom. 8:1). He bore our sins in his own body on the tree, suffering what we deserved so that we should never suffer what he suffered. We shall never be scapegoats or sin-offerings. We shall never plumb as he did the depths of spiritual dereliction: 'My God, my God, why hast thou forsaken me?' Surely the whole point of the cross is that his suffering secures our immunity?

Manson's interpretation simply will not allow us to do justice to the unique redemptive significance of the suffering and especially of the cross of Christ. In the New Testament the Lord's death is no accident or afterthought. It is more of the nature of a liturgy, patterned on the Old Testament *cultus* and presided over by God the Father. Its necessity is rooted in his nature. Its legitimacy is rooted in his command. It was a work given (John 17:4). It was the very purpose for which he came (John 12:27). He, given without limit or condition or qualification, was the supreme expression of God's love (Rom. 5:8; 8:32). He is also the pre-eminent and even the exclusive *locus* of God's redemptive achievement. In him, God expiates, propitiates, reconciles, redeems and justifies. All of these actions are uniquely related to Christ. We are righteous in him (2 Cor. 5:21). We have redemption in him (Eph. 1:7). He is himself our propitiation (1 John 2:2), by his one sacrifice perfecting his people for ever (Heb. 10:14).

We have no wish to deny either the reality or the value of Christian suffering. But it is never in the New Testament sense redemptive. It does not avail as a ransom. Nor does the New Testament ever apply to it any of the great words mentioned above: expiation, propitiation, reconciliation, justification. Christian suffering is incidental to Christian service and that service is not piacular but responsive: a response to the mercies of God (Rom. 12:1). This is not to minimise its pain or to say that there is no sense in which Christians suffer for the world. There is pain in intercession, there is pain in preaching and there is pain in martyrdom. But whereas in Christ's case the dying was the very essence of his service (he came in order to give his life, Mark 10:45), in the Christian's case the dying is secondary. Paul's real vocation, for example, was to bear the Lord's name (Acts 9:15): the things he suffered were incidental to that. Besides, there is profound a-symmetry between what 'the saints of the Most High' suffer and what Christ suffered. He endured death with its sting. For the Christian, that sting is drawn (1 Cor. 15:55).

We cannot, however, leave the matter there. There is truth, and great truth, in the idea of the Corporate Christ. Even though it cannot be deduced from the title *the Son of Man* it can be found elsewhere in the New Testament. According to Hebrews 2:14, for example, Christ shares our nature; according to Hebrews 4:15, he shared our experiences and can still be touched with the feeling of our infirmities; and according to Galatians 2:20, Christ by his Spirit indwells us and lives in us. We, for our own part, live as people-in-Christ. We are members of his body, sustained by his vitality and directed by him as Head. Conversely, he is afflicted in our afflictions and persecuted in our persecutions (Acts 9:5). As Priest, he is our Representative. As Sacrifice, he is our Substitute. In him we obeyed, just as in Adam we disobeyed (Rom. 5:19).

Yet all the language used to describe and define the Corporate Christ presupposes that he is quite distinct from his people. He is *in* them, not identical with them. Nor is the distinction merely numerical, he being one being and they another. It is a qualitative distinction and, as such, an immeasurable one. As revelation unfolds, there is a remarkable parallel between the relation of the saints to the Son of Man and the relation of the kingdoms of the world to the Danielic figure. In Daniel 7:14, all peoples, nations and languages *worship* the Son of Man. In the New Jerusalem, 'There shall no more be anything accursed, but the throne of God and of the Lamb shall be in it, and his Servants shall worship Him' (Rev. 22:3). The Corporate Christ remains the Holy Other.

The Messianic Secret

Many (indeed almost all) scholars link the designation *Son of Man* to the concept of the Messianic Secret. It was, they say, a cryptic and ambiguous title, free from the taint of unacceptable Messianism. It did not in itself make any claims or expose the Lord to any charges.

There must be some truth in a judgement supported by so many prestigious names. But it leaves one uneasy. When we look at the contexts in which the Lord used the title we find that any ambiguity in the designation itself is more than counter-balanced by the explicitness of the predicates he attaches to it. The real issue is whether the title was understood by his hearers as a self-designation. The evidence suggests that it was, even by those who did not belong to the circle of disciples. For example, when the Lord said, 'The Son of man has power on earth to forgive sins' (Mark 2:10) there was nothing cryptic about either the claim or the self-reference. Conversely, when he said that the Son of Man had nowhere to lay his head (Luke 9:58) the self-reference cannot be in doubt; nor is there anything ambiguous in what he says about himself. In fact in some contexts the impact of the saying depended on its being clearly understood that he was making stupendous claims for himself. This is true, for example, in Mark 8:38: 'Whoever is ashamed of me and of my words, of him will the Son of Man be ashamed.'

We also find the Lord using the title when there was no need for secrecy. At Caesarea Philippi, for instance, there was no one present but disciples and the time had come, in the Lord's judgement, when they must be taught as explicitly as possible the fate that awaited their Master. Yet the designation he chose was *the Son of Man* and Peter's reaction makes plain that the Lord made his meaning perfectly clear (Mark 8:31f.). In fact, most of the Son of Man sayings occur after Caesarea Philippi; and most are uttered in the presence of the disciples. It is remarkable, too, that the Lord should use the title at his trial (Mark 14:62), when no secrecy was called for; and no less remarkable that so far as those judging him were concerned, there was, to say the least, no veiling of his meaning: 'Why do we still need witnesses? You have heard the blasphemy!' (Mark 14:63f.).

The whole idea of the Messianic secret probably needs careful reconsideration. For the moment, suffice it to say that this concept cannot serve as an explanation for the Lord's choice of *the Son of Man* as his preferred self-designation. The title never obscured his meaning or his claims. Peter knew what the Lord meant and so did Caiaphas. We shall probably never know the precise reasons behind our Lord's choice. Maybe he was attracted to it by a process of elimination. The other titles available (the Messiah, the Lord, the Son of David) were either compromised theologically and politically or psychologically difficult (as we have seen, *Lord* is more appropriate as a form of address than as a self-designation).

But the Danielic associations of the title must not be forgotten. Our Lord, we are told, was sustained by the joy set before him (Heb. 12:2) and *the Son of Man* was a reminder of that. One day, his people would receive a kingdom at his hand; and one day, all peoples, nations and languages would serve him. But even in the midst of such thoughts the idea of the Suffering Servant could never be very far away: 'He shall see the travail of his soul and shall be satisfied' (Isa. 53:11).

References

1. J. Calvin, *Commentary on the Gospel According to John* (Edinburgh: Calvin Translation Society, 1847), Vol. I, p. 120.

2. D.R. Jackson, "The Priority of the Son of Man Sayings" (*Westminster Theological Journal*, Vol. XLVII, 1985), pp. 83-96.

3. B. Lindars, *Jesus Son of Man* (London: SPCK, 1983), p. 17.

4. P. M.. Casey, *Aramaic Idiom and Son of Man Sayings* (*Expository Times*, Vol. 96, No. 8, p. 233).

5. B. Lindars, *Jesus Son of Man*, p. 17.

6. B. Lindars, *op. cit.*, pp. 29-59.

7. B Lindars, *op. cit.*, p. 34.

8. G. Vos, *The Self-Disclosure of Jesus*, p. 50.

9. G. Vos, *op. cit.*, p. 51.

10. B. Lindars, *Jesus Son of Man*, p. 52.

11. P.M. Casey, *op. cit.*, p. 235.

12. Morna D Hooker, *The Son of Man in Mark* (London: SPCK, 1967), p. 186.

13. P.M. Casey, *op. cit.*, p. 236.

14. B. Lindars, *op. cit.*, p. 21.

15. B. Lindars, *op. cit.*, p. 161.

16. T.W. Manson, *The Teaching of Jesus* (Cambridge: Cambridge University Press, 1935), p. 212.

17. C.S. Lewis, *Fern-seed and Elephants* (Glasgow: Collins [Fontana Books], p. 112.

18. C.F.D. Moule, *op. cit.*, pp. 11-22.

19. B Lindars, *op. cit.*, p. 11.

20. G. Vos, *op. cit.*, p. 233.

21. G. Vos, *op. cit.*, p. 236.

22. G. Vos, *op. cit.*, p. 237.

23. E.J. Young, *A Commentary on Daniel* (London: Banner of Truth Trust, 1972), p. 156.

24. T.W. Manson, *The Teaching of Jesus*, p. 212.

25. T.W. Manson, *op. cit.*, p. 227.

26. C.F.D. Moule, *The Phenomenon of the New Testament* (London: SCM Press, 1967), p. 35.

27. M.D. Hooker, *The Son of Man in Mark*, pp. 27 ff.

28. C.F.D. Moule, *The Origin of Christology*, pp. 14 ff.

29. T.W. Manson, *op. cit.*, p. 229.

30. T.W. Manson, *op. cit.*, p. 231.

4

GOD OR GOD?:
ARIANISM ANCIENT AND MODERN*

Belief in the deity of Jesus Christ is well warranted by the canonical Scriptures of the Christian church. When we move, however, from exegesis and biblical theology to the realm of systematic reflection we soon find ourselves struggling. In what sense is Jesus *God*? This question was raised in an acute form by the Arian controversy of the fourth century. The church gave what it hoped were definitive answers in the Nicene Creed of 325 and the Nicaeno-Constantinopolitan Creed of 381, but, despite these, Arianism persisted long after the death of the heresiarch.

This chapter focuses on later British Arianism, particularly the views of the great Evangelical leaders, Isaac Watts and Philip Doddridge.

Arius

It is a commonplace that history has been unkind to heretics. In the case of such men as Praxeas and Pelagius we know virtually nothing of their teaching except what we can glean from the voluminous writings of their opponents (notably Tertullian and Augustine). Arius (probably born in Libya around 256, died 336) is in little better case. References to him in the works of such adversaries as Athanasius need to be treated with the greatest care, not least because the reputation of Athanasius the Great is not what it used to be. Recent scholarship has raised serious questions as to his personal integrity. R. P. C. Hanson, for example, accuses him of equivocation, mendacity, sharp practice and treason,[1] and this generally unfavourable verdict is endorsed by other contemporary scholars such as Professor Rowan Williams.[2] It is doubtful if these judgements express the last word on this particular

---

*This article first appeared in *The Evangelical Quarterly* (Vol. LXVII, No. 2, April, 1996), pp. 121-38.

Christian hero, but they certainly underline our misfortune in having so little direct knowledge of what his opponents, especially Arius, actually taught. As Hanson points out[3] the heresiarch himself wrote only ephemera, his alleged heirs and successors hardly ever quoted him and 'we have no more than three letters, a few fragments of another, and what purport to be long quotations from the *Thalia*, verses written in the Sotadean metre or style to set forth his doctrines'. Among his early supporters were the historian Eusebius of Caesarea and his namesake Eusebius of Nicomedia. In the next generation something very similar to Arius' views were set forth by Eunomius, calling forth a massive reply from Gregory of Nyssa.[4]

Recent scholarship has also been much less confident than that of the past as to what Arianism actually was.[5] Gibbon, in a famous jibe, made fun of the church dividing over an iota, as if the point at issue was whether Christ was consubstantial (*homoousios*) with God or merely like (*homoiousios*) him. But this was not the question at Nicea. Arius rejected *homoiousios* as firmly as he did *homoousios* and held instead that the Son was *heteroousios* (of another and alien substance from the Father). Whether there ever was a party using the slogan *homoiousios* is open to doubt. The label is certainly attached to a particular party in the Second Sirmian Creed, but the men in question (such as Basil of Ancyra) do not appear to have used it themselves. They preferred to speak of the Son as the image (*eikon*) of the *ousia* or as *homoios kat' ousian* ('similar in substance'). The position is further complicated by the fact that Athanasius himself uses *eikon* and occasionally (even after Nicea) *homoios*. Only later did these terms become party labels.

Whatever the uncertainties, however, it is clear that in the church of the early fourth century there was a substantial body of theological opinion which regarded the Son as a creature, produced in time, out of nothing, and distinguished from other creatures only by his existing before this world was made and by his being indwelt by the Logos in a unique way. As far as his nature went, he was utterly different from God.[6]

Anglican Arianism

By the close of the fourth century this school of opinion had been effectively excommunicated from the church. But it has never been totally extinguished. As far as the Western church is concerned it reared its head again after the Reformation, not least in England, although early English Arians tended to be inconsequential figures who simply reproduced the arguments of their more substantial Continental counterparts. The most important of these was the Dutch Socinian, Sandius, who reproduced the argument of the Jesuit Petavius to the effect that the ante-Nicene fathers would not have supported the terms of the Nicene Creed. Petavius' own trinitarianism is not in question: his concern was to establish the right of the church (that is, the Roman Catholic Church) to formulate new doctrines. But his argument obviously suited Arians well since it allowed them to present orthodoxy as a late novelty. Sandius' arguments were taken up by several forgotten figures in English theology, such as Dr. Bury of Exeter College, whose book *The Naked Gospel* was published at Oxford in 1690.

It was to refute the thesis of Petavius and Sandius that George Bull, later Bishop of St. Davids (Menavia, in Wales) published in 1685 his *Defence of the Nicene Faith* (the original title was, of course, in Latin). Bull sought to establish one point, namely, that 'what the Nicene fathers laid down concerning the divinity of the Son, in opposition to Arius and other heretics, the same in effect (although sometimes, it may be, in another mode of expression) was taught, without any single exception, by all the fathers and approved doctors of the Church, who flourished before the Council of Nice, even from the very times of the Apostles.'[7]

Effective as Bull's *Defence* was, however, the controversy continued. Thinkers such as William Whiston, who succeeded Isaac Newton as Professor of Mathematics at Cambridge, continued to propound Arian views (Whiston was deprived of his professorship for his pains). Various Anglican dignitaries, endeavouring to clarify the Nicene teaching, found that their subtle speculations served only to raise questions as to their own orthodoxy. Dr. Robert South accused Dr. William Sherlock of tritheism, only to find himself accused in turn of Sabellianism. In the University of Oxford Sherlock's views were publicly banned and prohibited. This produced further irritation 'and such was the unbecoming heat and acrimony with which the controversy was conducted, that the Royal Authority was at last exercised, in restraining each party from introducing novel opinions respecting these mysterious articles of faith, and requiring them to such explications only, as had already received the sanction of the Church'.[8]

But trinitarianism soon faced a more formidable adversary in the person of Dr. Samuel Clarke, a London Rector, who published his *Scripture Doctrine of the Trinity* in 1712. Clarke did not regard himself as anti-trinitarian and to some extent his objections to orthodox doctrine were methodological rather than substantial. He rejected the authority of the Fathers on such matters and argued that everyone, including Arians, should be allowed to subscribe to the formularies of the Church of England in his own sense. 'Every person,' he wrote, 'may reasonably agree to such forms, whenever he can *in any sense at all reconcile them with Scripture*.'[9] More important, Clarke distinguished between *god* and the *supreme God*. Christ was god, but he was not the supreme God. The Son was divine only in so far as divinity could be communicated by the Father, who alone is unoriginated and is the final source and first cause of all that the Son and Spirit do.[10]

The Arian tendencies of Clarke's position were quickly recognised and his work was condemned by Convocation in 1714. But this failed to settle the dispute. Others, notably Daniel Whitby, took up a position similar to Clarke's; and orthodoxy found an outstanding champion in Daniel Waterland (1683-1740).[11]

Arianism in Scotland

Unsettledness on the doctrine of the trinity was not confined to Anglicanism, however. The Church of Scotland, too, had its problems. John Simson, Professor of Divinity at Glasgow University, was accused of denying the necessary existence of Christ at three successive General Assemblies between 1727 and 1729. When the Assembly finally shrank from deposing him

Thomas Boston dissented, on the ground that the decision failed to express 'this Church's indignation against the dishonour done by the said Mr. Simson to our glorious Redeemer, the great God and our Saviour'.[12] The failure to deal with Simson's Arianism was also one of the grievances which led to a substantial secession from the Church of Scotland in 1733.[13]

Arianism in Nonconformity

But far more serious developments were taking place in English Nonconformity, where Arianism spread rapidly in the eighteenth century. The reasons for this lay, largely, in the historical context. Dissenters inherited from such men as Richard Baxter an aversion to 'human impositions', and this was exacerbated by the disabilities imposed on them by the Test Act (passed by Parliament in 1673), which bred a loathing of all theological tests and led to a reluctance to subscribe to even the most ancient creeds of the church. Along with this went a passion for theological freedom and a general feeling that churches must reserve to themselves a total liberty to reform their doctrine, worship and discipline according to the Scriptures.

To all this was added the confused and disorganised state of nonconformist churches, particularly the presbyterians. Presbyteries found themselves unable to exercise proper supervision over preachers and congregations and even less able to supervise theological education, which was conducted for the most part in private academies. Even the laws governing the ownership of Dissenting churches contributed to the problem. Every such property had to be vested in a trustee, and these trustees tended to be wealthy laymen, reluctant to incorporate any theological statement into their trust deeds, and stipulating only that the building be used 'for the worship of God by Protestant Dissenters'. Add the influence of Anglican Arianism, plus the cold rationalism introduced into English religion by John Locke, and it becomes easy to understand how Arianism could make rapid progress even among the heirs of the Puritans.

By 1718 matters had become so critical that the problem was referred to a Leaders' Conference.[14] This 'Salters' Hall

Conference', as it came to be called, debated a proposal that ministers be required to subscribe to a traditional orthodox formula. Tragically, the Conference divided into 'subscribers' and 'non-subscribers': a division which marked a watershed in the history of Nonconformity. By the end of the century there were two hundred Unitarian chapels in England and the movement as a whole had acquired significant influence through such men as Joseph Priestley (1733-1804), whose spiritual pilgrimage saw him move from Calvinism to Arminianism to Arianism. Priestley's *Appeal to the Serious and Candid Professors of Christianity* was published in London in 1770.

Isaac Watts

Among the non-subscribers at the Salters' Hall Conference was Isaac Watts. David Fountain dismisses the question of Watts' views on the trinity in less than a page (and an even briefer appendix),[15] but this does not do justice either to the labour Watts bestowed on this doctrine or to the suspicion it aroused.[16] Watts' output on the subject of the trinity occupies almost the whole of Volume VI of his collected works (nearly six hundred closely printed pages). That is surely sufficient to allow a balanced assessment of his position.

Watts clearly saw himself as an orthodox trinitarian. For example, he applauded the work of Bull, Pearson and Waterland: 'I reverence the name and memory of Bishop Bull, and Bishop Pearson, whose excellent writings have effectually proved, that those primitive fathers did generally believe the true and eternal Deity of Christ. And I pay all due honours to the learned labours of the reverend Doctor Waterland.'[17] In accordance with this, his work, *The Christian Doctrine of the Trinity*, abounds with citations from these authorities. It is clear, too, that Watts was fully aware of the defects of Arianism and argued strongly against it: 'it is that scheme which represents the blessed Jesus as an inferior god, and thus brings him too near to the rank of those inferior gods or heroes in the sense of the heathens; whereas the scripture places him in a vastly superior character, as *God over all blessed for ever*, and as one with God the Father.'[18] Nor does Watts leave us in any doubt as to his personal belief in the Deity of Christ: 'since the studies of these last years I think I am established afresh in the belief of the Deity of Christ, and the blessed Spirit, and assured of it upon sufficient grounds, that they are one with the Father in godhead, though they are represented in scripture as distinct persons.'[19] In accordance with this Watts argues, over many pages, that divine names, titles, attributes, works and worship are ascribed by the New Testament to Christ.[20]

Yet it is easy to see why Watts' attempts to explain and defend his position brought him under suspicion. He had a curiously conciliatory approach to Arianism: 'I would not,' he wrote, 'willingly call every man an enemy to Christ, who lies under some doubts of his supreme godhead.'[21] He was also reluctant to confront Arianism head-on and sought instead to lead those who held Arian sentiments to belief in the divinity of Christ by 'soft and easy steps';[22] and in the process of doing so he always felt bound to reassure them that he did not expect them to accept the whole orthodox package. In a typical statement he wrote: 'Now I ask leave to try whether it is not possible to lead one who has favoured Arian sentiments toward belief of *the chief parts of this doctrine*, which for some ages past has obtained the name of orthodoxy, though I confess *there are some other parts of it which are not so defensible.*'[23]

Watts also shared, of course, the aversion to credal formulations and theological tests which was prevalent among the Dissenters of his day. This explains why he took his position with the non-subscribers at the Salters' Hall Conference. It explains, too, his consistent reluctance to endorse the details of historical orthodoxy: 'as to the various particular explications of this doctrine, and incidental arguments that attend it, I desire to believe and to write with a humble consciousness of my own ignorance, and to give my assent but in proportion to the degrees of light and evidence'.[24] The same reluctance to commit himself to traditional formulations appears in Watts' attitude to the personality of the Holy Spirit. He felt quite free to speculate on this question: 'the Spirit seems to be another divine power, which may be called the Spirit of efficience: And though it is sometimes described in scripture as a personal agent, after the manner of Jewish and eastern writers, yet if we put all the scriptures relating to this subject together, and view them in a corresponding light, the Spirit of God does not seem to be described as a distinct spirit from the Father, or as another conscious mind, but as an eternal essential power, belonging to the Father, whereby all things are effected.'[25]

But the real problem lay in Watts' speculations on the Person of the Son. He had serious misgivings about the eternal sonship of Christ: 'Though it has been an opinion generally received, that the sonship of Christ belongs to his divine nature, supposing it to be really derived from the Father by eternal generation, yet the scripture does nowhere assert this doctrine, but it is drawn only by supposed consequences.'[26] Along with this went a peculiar belief in the pre-existence of the human soul of Christ. Watts regarded this as the most natural and obvious sense of many Scriptures and he even expressed his opinion in language reminiscent of the fourth century Arians: 'if we can believe that it was formed the first of creatures before the foundation of the world, and was present with God in the beginning of all things, which is no hard matter for an Arian to grant, then we may also justly believe this union between God and man to have begun before the world was, in some unknown moment of God's own eternity.'[27] It was in this sense, Watts asserted, that Christ was the first-born of every creature: 'For his complex person had a being before the creation was formed; and, perhaps, this may be the best way of expounding the doctrine of the most primitive fathers concerning the ante-mundane generation of Christ, that is, his becoming the Son of God in a new manner just before the world was made.'[28] This involved the idea that 'his person as God-man existed before the foundation of the world',[29] which in turn explained how, as God-man, he had some hand in creation. To complete the picture, 'The human soul of Christ being thus anciently united to the divine nature, did about seventeen hundred years ago, assume a body that was prepared for it by the Father through the peculiar operation of the Holy Spirit.'[30]

Wow! We must remember the motivation behind this treatise, entitled *The Arian Invited to the Orthodox Faith*. In it, Watts was struggling to find common ground with Arianism, to be as conciliatory as possible and to meet Arian scruples as far as he could. But even J. A. Dorner was astonished, declaring, 'From this view to Arianism was but a short step.'[31] Watts, however, did not take that step. Instead he saw his position as depriving Arianism of its force, because it allowed him to argue that all apparently subordinationist references to Christ applied only to his pre-existent human soul. The underlying problem was that in his determination to avoid bondage to ancient credal formularies Watts embarked upon the very kind of speculation which had made these formularies necessary in the first place.[32]

Philip Doddridge

The name of Philip Doddridge is often bracketed with that of Isaac Watts in discussions of English Arianism. For example, in a letter to Dr. James Denney, Sir William Robertson Nicoll asked Denney whether he had read the history of Arianism and went on to say : 'I read it up pretty fully a long time ago. There is a meagre and not very accurate account of it in Dorner. Briefly, there was a powerful section led by Watts and Doddridge in the 18th century. They endeavoured to find a middle term between Trinitarianism and Arianism.'[33] Referring more particularly to Doddridge, Nicoll declared: 'As for Doddridge, he was virtually, I think, an Arian. At least, he recognised the Arians as brothers, though he admitted some modifications. Principal Gordon, who is biased but well informed, says that the majority of Doddridge's students became Arians, and he is rather disposed to think that Doddridge himself was.'

Unfortunately, Nicoll does not document his claims. Doddridge's treatment of the trinity and related issues is much less extensive than that of Watts, and it is presented at two different levels: the popular and the academic.

The popular is found in the *Family Expositor*, a paraphrase and exposition of the New Testament written towards the end of Doddridge's life[34] and designed, in his own words, to 'promote family religion'. The format gave Doddridge an excellent opportunity to express his opinion of the key texts on the deity of

Christ and in every instance his exposition is unashamedly, indeed aggressively, orthodox. For example, writing on Acts 20:28 he rejects the variant kuriou (for qeou) and declares, 'this passage must be allowed as an incontestable proof that *the blood of Christ* is here called *the blood of God*, as being *the blood of that man who is also God with us, God manifest in the flesh.*'[35] He writes to similar effect on Romans 9:5, arguing that there is no authority for the rendering, 'God who is over all be blessed for ever!' and asserting that the passage is 'a proof of *Christ's proper Deity*, which I think the opposers of that doctrine have never been able, nor will ever be able, to answer'.[36]

The strongest comments, however, are to be found in Doddridge's notes on John 1:1. Here he faces the argument of Clarke and others that the word qeos is used in some inferior sense (*god* rather than *God*). His response is emphatic: 'it is to me most incredible that, when the Jews were so exceedingly averse to idolatry, and the Gentiles so unhappily prone to it, such a plain writer as this apostle should lay so dangerous a stumbling-block on the very threshold of his work, and represent it as the Christian doctrine, that *in the beginning* of all things there were *two gods*, one supreme and the other subordinate.'[37]

However, Doddridge also appears to be aware that he himself had been suspected of holding the very sentiments repudiated in his exposition. He replies with feeling: 'Nothing I have said above can, by any means, be justly interpreted in such a sense; and I here solemnly disclaim the least intention of insinuating one thought of that kind, by anything I have ever written, here or elsewhere.'[38]

Doddridge's more academic pronouncements on the doctrine of the trinity are to be found in his two-volume *Course of Lectures on the Principal Subjects in Pneumatology, Ethics and Divinity.* Here, again, he argues cogently for the pre-existence of Christ and, like Watts, enumerates in proof of Christ's divinity the divine names, titles, attributes, works and honours which are ascribed to him in the New Testament, concluding that 'such divine worship is required or encouraged to him, as is elsewhere appropriated to the one eternal and ever-blessed God'.[39]

On closer examination, however, it becomes easy to understand why Doddridge fell under the suspicion of heresy.

In the first place, although in these lectures the arguments for Christ's Deity are clearly stated, the relation between him and the divine nature remains ambiguous: 'God is so *united* to the derived nature of Christ, and does so dwell in it, that by virtue of that *union* Christ may be properly called *God*, and such regards become due to him, as are not due to any *created* nature, or mere creature, be it in itself ever so excellent.'[40]

Secondly, Doddridge endorsed Watts' idea of the pre-existence of the human soul of Christ: 'there is reason to believe that Christ had before his incarnation a *created* or *derived* nature ... though we are far from saying he had *no other* nature.'[41] It is of this being, possessed of a derived or created nature, that Doddridge speaks as 'this glorious spirit or Logos'[42] to whom Scripture ascribes the work of creation. It is not clear whether the Logos had a distinct personal existence prior to his union with the created nature or whether the Logos is only the result of the Father's uniting himself to this created nature.

Thirdly, Doddridge gave the impression of being uncommitted on the question of the *personality* of the Holy Spirit. He contents himself with summarising the arguments of those who assert, on the one hand, that the Spirit is a *person* and of those who assert, on the other, that he is but a divine *power*.[43]

Fourthly, Doddridge deliberately cultivated an indefinite, non-dogmatic style of theological teaching. His general practice was to list for students the various views that had been held on a given question, refer them to the relevant literature and leave them to decide for themselves. Joseph Priestley, who studied under Doddridge's pupil, Caleb Ashworth, recalled the experience with relish: 'The general plan of our studies, which may be seen in Dr Doddridge's published lectures, was exceedingly favourable to free enquiry, as we were referred to authors on both sides of every question, and were then required to give an account of them.'[44]

This, of course, is the standard approach in modern academic institutions. But these are secular institutions, where neutrality on the part of the teacher and free enquiry on the part of the student are *de rigeur*. Doddridge worked in a totally different environment, where he was charged with training men for the ministry and expected to give them clear guidance on fundamental Christian doctrines; and where dogmatism on such matters as the Deity of Christ and the personality of the Holy Spirit would have been accepted as a matter of course. If, in such an environment, he pursued a course completely different from that of a Calvin, an Athanasius or a St Paul, it is tempting to conclude either that he did not have firm views of his own or that he did not think orthodoxy important, even on fundamental doctrines. It is one thing for a ministerial academy to encourage open-mindedness on the distinctives of Calvinism and the peculiarities of Baxterianism. It is quite something else to encourage such liberalism with regard to the Trinity. The fact that the trinitarian controversy was at its height during Doddridge's student days and continued throughout his life[45] serves only to make his muted pronouncements all the more surprising.

Finally, and most important of all, Doddridge seems to have been governed throughout his life by an overriding concern to maintain his theological freedom; and, as a corollary to this, by a profound aversion to human creeds. In this, he was, of course, following in the footsteps of later Puritans such as Richard Baxter and (to a lesser extent) John Howe.[46] This attitude is reflected in many aspects of Doddridge's life and ministry. He could have had a place at either Oxford or Cambridge but declined because he could not conform to Anglicanism. In 1723, when he became a minister in Leicestershire, he did not accept ordination or subscribe to any statement of faith.[47] In 1724 he declined to become a candidate for the pastorate of Girdlers' Hall, London, because the position involved subscribing to the (Westminster) Assembly's Catechism.[48] And while his *Lectures* certainly describe Arianism as a heresy[49] the *homoousion* received only the barest mention and the post-Nicene fathers are damned with faint praise. 'After the time of this celebrated council,' he writes, 'they ran into several subtilties of expression, in which one would imagine they studied rather to conceal than to explain their sentiments'.[50] Doddridge rightly deprecated the squalid feuding which was such a feature of the fourth century Arian controversy, but he does not seem to have grasped the gravity of what was at stake. His conclusion tells us more about himself than it does about the subject: 'Considering the excellent character of many of the persons abovementioned, whose opinions were most widely different, we may assure ourselves, that many things asserted on the one side and on the other relating to the trinity, are not fundamental in religion.... We may hence learn to be cautious, how we enter into unscriptural niceties in expressing our own conceptions on this doctrine, which is by all allowed to be so sublime and so peculiar to revelation.'[51]

Subscription
Doddridge gave a formal deliverance on the question of subscription to human Forms and Standards in *Part VIII, Proposition CXXXVIII* of his *Lectures*.[52] He rejected the practice for five reasons: first, if such Forms had been necessary Scripture itself would have provided them; secondly, it is inconceivable that 'weak and passionate' men could express themselves more appropriately than the apostles; thirdly, far from bringing unity, such formularies had brought great division to the church; fourthly, they would deter those who had the greatest tenderness of conscience (the very kind of men the church needed); and, fifthly, they would not secure the desired uniformity of belief because men of little integrity would subscribe to them for the sake of remaining in the church, even if this meant 'putting the most unnatural sense on the words'.

This is plausible and, no doubt, honest. But it remains unconvincing. First, it represents an attempt to escape from history. Arius posed a question (indeed a series of questions) to which every subsequent generation of Christians must reply: what is the relation between God the Son and God the Father? Is he different in essence (*heteroousios*) or is he one and the same in essence (*homoousios*)? Is he begotten, or is he made? Is he a creature, or is he the Creator? Did he have a beginning, or is he eternal? These questions form part of the context of Christian theology not only in the fourth century, but in all ages afterwards. They were certainly part of the context in which Doddridge worked in the eighteenth century.

The historic answer to Arius was given in the Nicene Creed and this, too, remains an enduring part of our theological context. We need to discriminate, however. Doddridge, as we have seen, was less than fulsome in his praise of the Nicene Fathers, but no one was (or is) expected to subscribe to all the sentiments of such men as Athanasius and the Cappadocians. Subscription is to the Creed alone. That Creed gave a clear answer to Arius: Christ was begotten, not made; he was begotten of the Father's essence, not of his will; he was the Creator of all things in heaven and earth; and he was *homoousios* with the Father.

The question being put to Doddridge was not simply, 'Do you believe in the Deity of Christ?' but, 'Are you on the side of Arius or on the side of Nicea?' It is hardly surprising that his attempt to distance himself from both sides (although not equally) brought him under suspicion.

Secondly, Doddridge's attitude reflects an excessive individualism. He recognised that a congregation had a right to know, for example, the theological position of its pastor, and when he himself was ordained at Northampton in March, 1730, he drafted a Confession of his own faith. It was, however, emphatically personal.[53] It was not one of the great ecumenical creeds or one of the great Protestant confessions or even a statement drafted by the congregation itself. It was entirely individual.

The difficulty with this is that the church is a community and that the study of theology is a communal activity. Certainly, the paramount consideration is whether the preacher's words accord with those of the prophets and the apostles. But if he is at all competent theologically he has also studied with the Fathers and with the Reformers and with the theological community down through the ages and all over the world. Is he unable to express his agreement (and acknowledge his debt) in a common Formula? And is his church so distinctive that it needs a creed all its own?

Thirdly, Doddridge's approach reflects a simplistic biblicism. There is nothing whatever in the Reformation slogan, *sola scriptura,* to preclude the use of creeds and confessions in the church.[54] In fact, Doddridge himself repeatedly used non-biblical language, including some of the technical terms with which he was so uneasy. He affirmed, for example, his belief in the *trinity* (a non-biblical word) and even used the concepts *substance* and *person*. Besides, the New Testament itself, in the judgement of modern New Testament scholarship, contains several confessions of faith which were quoted (rather than composed) by the writers of the Epistles and which circulated as a 'form (j}upotuposis) of sound words' (2 Tim. 1:13) before the completion of the canon. There is good evidence that Philippians 2:5-11 represents such a creed, that Romans 1:3f. represents another and that 1 Timothy 3:16 represents yet another.[55] If this is so, then the practice of creed-making has clear apostolic sanction. Provided such creeds are drafted in submission to Scripture and live under its constant scrutiny they pose no threat to the authority of the canon. After all, it was one of the greatest of all creed-composing gatherings, the Westminster Assembly, which declared that, 'the Word of God, given in the scriptures of the Old and New Testaments, is the *only* rule to direct us' (*Westminster Shorter Catechism,* Answer 2).

But the real difficulty with Doddridge's appeal to the sufficiency of Scripture is that the writers of the New Testament never faced the precise issues raised by Arianism and therefore made no pronouncement upon it. This is further complicated by the fact that the very point at issue was the meaning of the biblical statements about Jesus. What did John mean when he said that the Logos was *God*? Or Paul, when he said that Christ was 'the first-born of all creation'? Such questions could not be answered by the mechanical citation of biblical texts. They required clear answers as to the way the texts were understood. From this point of view, nothing could be more serviceable than the *homoousion*, a hermeneutical axiom which forbids any exegesis inconsistent with the fact that Christ has the same divine nature, functions and prerogatives as God the Father.[56] We cannot object to the use of the idea of substance (*ousia*) merely on the ground that it is unbiblical. The Arians themselves introduced the idea of substance by arguing that Christ was of a different substance from the Father.

It was entirely appropriate that the orthodox should counter this in cognate terminology, insisting that Christ was one and the same in substance with the Father.[57]

Finally, Doddridge's attitude to doctrinal formulations (and particularly to the Nicene Creed) reflects a deficient sense of theological proportion. A Calvinist, such as Doddridge was, can be understandably uneasy about excluding from the ministry of the church an Arminian such as John Wesley or an Amyraldian such as Richard Baxter. Neither of these deviations from the Calvinist norm is life-threatening to the body of Christ. But Arianism (or Unitarianism) is a different order of error altogether. It illegitimates the worship of Christ. Doddridge does not seem to have reckoned with this difference in scale. In one of his letters he pays an oft-quoted tribute to a former teacher, John Jennings: 'He does not entirely accord with the system of any particular body of men; but is sometimes a Calvinist, sometimes a Remonstrant, sometimes a Baxterian, and sometimes a Socinian, as truth and evidence determine him'.[58] But this is inept. Arminianism and Socinianism (modern Arianism) do not belong together. Arianism deserved not Doddridge's languid tolerance but Athanasius' obsessive determination to expel it from the church.

Conclusion

It seems fair to conclude that Arianism, feeding on the plea for simplicity and riding on the band-wagon of protest against non-biblical jargon, is endemic to the church. The concept of God as undifferentiated monad will always have its appeal, while attempts to explain the relations between co-equal divine persons can easily be portrayed as special pleading. Yet, for all its plausibility, Arianism is fatal to Christianity. We cannot call a creature, however glorious, *Lord*! For this reason, Arianism falls outwith the range of theological pluralism tolerable within the church.

References

1. R.P.C. Hanson, *The Search for the Christian Doctrine of God* (Edinburgh: T & T Clark, 1988), pp. 244-246.

2. R. Williams in *The Scottish Journal of Theology*, Vol. 45, Number 1, p. 107 . Cf. Hans von Campenhausen, *The Fathers of the Greek Church* (London: SCM Press, 1963) p. 73.

3. R.P.C. Hanson, *op.cit.*, pp. 5 f.

4. Gregory of Nyssa, *Against Eunomius* (written between 381 and 384). See *The Nicene and Post-Nicene Fathers*, Second Series (Grand Rapids: Eerdmans, 1979), Vol. V, pp. 33-248.

5. R. Williams, *op. cit.*, p. 102.

6. See Athanasius, *Discourses against the Arians* and *Arian History*; J.N.D. Kelly, *Early Christian Doctrines* (Third Edition, London 1965), pp. 226-231; J.N.D. Kelly, *Early Christian Creeds* (Second Edition, London, 1965), pp. 231-234; R.P.C. Hanson, *The Search for the Christian Doctrine of God*, pp. 3-5; J.H. Newman, *The Arians of the Fourth Century* (London, 1890).

7. G. Bull, *A Defence of the Nicene Creed* (A New Translation, Oxford, 1852) pp. x-xi.

8. *The Works of the Rev. Daniel Waterland*, D.D. (Oxford, 1823), Vol. I, pp. 41-42. The quotation is from the *Review of Waterland's Life and Writings* prefixed to this edition.

9. Waterland, Vol. I, p. 45, quoting S. Clarke, *The Scripture Doctrine of the Trinity* (1712), p. 21.

10. See J.A. Dorner, *History of the Development of the Doctrine of the Person of Christ* (Edinburgh: T&T Clark, 1872), Vol. II, p. 358.

11. See Waterland's *Vindication of Christ's Divinity*, 1719; *Eight Sermons in Defence of the Divinity of Our Lord Jesus Christ*, 1720; *The Case of Arian Subscription Considered*, 1721; *Second Vindication of Christ's Divinity*, 1723; *Critical History of the Athanasian Creed*, 1723; *A Farther Vindication of Christ's Divinity*, 1724; and *The Importance of the Doctrine of the Holy Trinity Asserted*, 1734.

12. See Boston's *Memoirs* (Glasgow: New Edition, 1899), p. 402.

13. See Adam Gib, *Display of the Secession Testimony* (Edinburgh, 1744), Vol. I, p. 44.

14. See Cragg, *The Church and the Age of Reason* (London: Penguin, 1970), p. 137.

15. D. Fountain, *Isaac Watts Remembered* (Worthing, 1974), p. 79.

16. See Augustus Toplady's comment in his *Outlines of the Life of Dr. Isaac Watts*: 'Gladly would I throw, if possible, an everlasting veil over this valuable person's occasional deviations from the simplicity of the gospel, relative to the personality and divinity of the Son and Spirit of God. But justice compels me to acknowledge that he did not always preserve an uniform consistency with himself, nor with the scriptures of truth, so far as that grand and fundamental article of the Christian faith.... The inclusiveness (to call it by the tenderest name we can) of his too wanton tamperings with the doctrine of the Trinity, have been largely and irrefragably demonstrated by more hands than one.... Notwithstanding this declension, I am happy in believing that the grace and faithfulness of the Holy Ghost did not permit our author to die under the delusions of so horrible and pernicious a heresy' (London: *Works*, 1841), p. 487). Compare Dorner, *op. cit.*, pp. 330-333.

17. *The Works of the Rev. Isaac Watts*, D.D., (Leeds, 1813), Vol. VI, p. 274.

18. *Ibid.*, p. 250.

19. *Ibid.*, p. 210.

20. *Ibid.*, pp. 124 ff.

21. *Ibid.*, p. 211.

22. *Ibid.*, p. 225.

23. *Ibid.*, p. 215 (italics mine).

24. *Ibid.*, p. 210.

25. *Ibid.*, p. 341.

26. *Ibid.*, p. 220 fn.

27. *Ibid.*, p. 221.

28. *Ibid.*, p. 221.

29. *Ibid.*, p. 221.

30. *Ibid.*, p. 222.

31. J.A. Dorner, *op. cit.*, p. 331.

32. William Robertson Nicoll claimed that Watts went further than appears in his published works: 'Isaac Watts had a theory which is correctly described in Dorner. But I have read a posthumous book of his in the British Museum which goes further than that, and Lardner, a very fair-minded and scholarly man, declares that Watts became before his death completely Unitarian' (T.H. Barlow, *William Robertson Nicoll: Life and Letters* (London: Hodder and Stoughton, 1925), pp. 361-362).

33. *Ibid.*, p. 361.

34. The Preface to the first volume is dated 27 November, 1738. The last volume was published posthumously. Quotations in this article are from P. Doddridge, *The Family Expositor: or, A paraphrase and Version of the New Testament*, (Leeds: Five Volumes, 1810).

35. *The Family Expositor*, Vol. III, p. 210.

36. *Ibid.*, p. 472 fn.

37. *The Family Expositor*, Vol. I, p. 24.

38. *Ibid.*, p. 24.

39. P. Doddridge, *A Course of Lectures on the Principal Subjects in Pneumatology, Ethics and Divinity* (London: 4th Edition, 1799), Vol. II, p. 168.

40. *Ibid.*, p. 170.

41. *Ibid.*, p. 154.

42. *Ibid.*, p. 154.

43. *Ibid*, pp. 180-182.

44. Cited in G.F. Nuttall, Ed., *Philip Doddridge 1702-51: His Contribution to English Religion* (London: Independent Press, 1951), p. 132.

45. Nuttall, *op. cit.*, p. 133.

46. See Howe's comment in *A Calm Discourse of the Trinity in the Godhead*: 'I only wish these things might be considered and discoursed with less confidence and peremptory determination; with a greater awe of what is divine and sacred; and that we may confine ourselves to the plain words of Scripture in this matter, and be content therewith' (*Works*, Vol. V, p. 112).

47. Doddridge was ordained in March, 1730, on his moving to Northampton, but the confession of faith he then made has been described as 'not so much a creed to which a young man might assent, but an account of his experience after seven years in the ministry' (G.F. Nuttall (Ed.), *Philip Doddridge: His Contribution to English Religion*, London, 1951, p. 111).

48. Nuttall, *op. cit.*, p. 144.

49. P. Doddridge, *Lectures*, Vol. II, p. 190.

50. *Ibid.*, p. 189.

51. *Ibid.*, p. 194.

52. *Ibid.*, pp. 241-247.

53. Nuttall, *op. cit.*, p. 111.

54. Calvin wrestled with the problem of the use of non-biblical language in connection with the trinity in the *Institutes*, Book I, Ch. XIII, pp. 3-5. While insisting that we must speak of God as reverently as we think of him, he argued, nevertheless, that, 'If they call a foreign word one that cannot be shown to stand written syllable by syllable in Scripture, they are indeed imposing upon us an unjust law which condemns all interpretation not patched together out of the fabric of Scripture.' He also argued that the historic terminology 'becomes especially useful when the truth is to be asserted against false accusers, who evade it by their shifts' (quotations from Calvin: *Institutes of the Christian Religion*, Edited by John T. McNeill, Translated and Indexed by Ford Lewis Battles, Westminster Press, Philadelphia, 1960).

55. See, for example, Oscar Cullmann, *The Earliest Christian Confessions* (London: Lutterworth, 1949); J.N.D. Kelly, *Early Christian Creeds* (New York: Third Edition, Longman, 1972); pp. 1-29; C.E.B. Cranfield, *A Critical and Exegetical Commentary on the Epistle to the Romans*, Vol. I (Edinburgh: T & T Clark, 1975), p. 57; R.P. Martin, *An Early Christian Confession* (London: Tyndale Press, 1960); George W. Knight III, *The Pastoral Epistles: A Commentary on the Greek Text* (Grand Rapids: Eerdmans, 1992), p. 182 f. Martin's work refers to Philippians 2:5-11, but in a later publication, *Carmen Christi* (Cambridge, 1967) he espoused the prevailing view that Philippians 2:5-11 is *hymnic* in form. Cf. Peter T. O'Brien, *The Epistle to the Philippians: A Commentary on the Greek Text* (Grand Rapids: Eerdmans, 1991), pp. 186-193.

56. This does not mean that the *homoousion* itself is above scrutiny. It must be kept under constant review, in the same way as physics must be alert to the possibility that some day Einstein's theories of relativity may be superseded. In the meantime, however, both Einstein and the *homoousion* provide indispensable working hypotheses.

Similarly, the *homoousion* may undergo further clarification. See, for example, Donald Mackinnon's distinction between Christ as *homoousios* with the divine and Christ as mere *simulacrum* of the divine: 'if we say that Christ's invitation to the heavy laden is not a *simulacrum* of the divine invitation but is *in fact* that invitation made concrete, are we not involved in something very close to the *homoousion*?' (from an essay '"Substance" in Christology – a cross-bench view' in *Christ, Faith and History*, ed. Sykes and Clayton, Cambridge, 1972, p. 290). The same point can be made by distinguishing between Christ as *simulacrum* of the divine and Christ as *parousia* of the divine.

57. Cf. Donald Mackinnon: 'the question whether or not theology can dispense with the notion of substance is closely related to the question whether or not theology can dispense with propositions' (*op. cit.*, p. 289).

58. Quoted in Nuttall, *op. cit.*, p. 132.

5

THE DOCTRINE OF THE INCARNATION IN SCOTTISH THEOLOGY

There was no distinctive Scottish Christology until the emergence of Edward Irving in the middle of the nineteenth century. Nor was there much Christological controversy: certainly nothing comparable to the Arianism which disturbed the church in England in the late seventeenth and early eighteenth centuries, calling forth the works of Bull, Waterland and Pearson. The closest parallel was the case of John Simson, Professor of Divinity at Glasgow University, who was accused of heresy at successive General Assemblies between 1727 and 1729. The specific charge against Simson was that he denied the necessary existence of Christ. When the General Assembly of 1729 shrank from deposing him Thomas Boston dissented, on the ground that the decision failed to express 'this Church's indignation against the dishonour done by the said Mr Simson to our glorious Redeemer, the great God and our Saviour'.[1] The failure to deal with Simson's Arianism was also one of the grievances which led to the Secession of 1733.[2] As far as Adam Gib was concerned, Simson was guilty of blasphemously impugning and denying the deity of the Lord Jesus Christ.[3]

But the Simson case closed with the 1729 Assembly. Serious Christological controversy began in Scotland only in 1828, when Edward Irving published *The Doctrine of the Incarnation Opened in Six Sermons*.[4] Irving's central tenet was that in becoming incarnate Christ took *fallen* human nature. Otherwise, he would not have been one with us; more particularly, he could not have been tempted.

Further publications followed, setting forth the same view: *The Orthodox and Catholic Doctrine of our Lord's Human Nature* in 1830 and *Christ's Holiness in Flesh* in 1831. As a result Irving

---

This is an expanded version of my article, 'Christology' in the *Dictionary of Scottish Church History and Theology* (Ed. N.M. de S. Cameron, Edinburgh: T & T Clark, 1993), pp. 172-77.

was charged with denying the sinlessness of Christ and deposed from the ministry in 1833.

Many have questioned this judgement. It merits three comments.

First, even those who were most disturbed by Irving's teaching respected his piety and acknowledged his devotion to Christ. Robert Murray McCheyne, for example, noted in his Diary for November 9, 1834: 'Heard of Edward Irving's death. I look back upon him with awe, as on the saints and martyrs of old. A holy man in spite of all his delusions and errors. He is now with his God and Saviour, whom he wronged so much, yet, I am persuaded, loved so sincerely.' A huge crowd attended his funeral and no one thought it incongruous that the preacher took as his text 2 Samuel 3:38, 'Know ye not that there is a prince and a great man fallen this day in Israel?'

Secondly, Irving himself vehemently affirmed his belief in the sinlessness of Jesus. 'I believe it to be necessary unto salvation,' he wrote, 'that a man should believe that Christ's soul was so held in possession by the Holy Ghost, and so supported by the divine nature, as that it never assented unto a single evil suggestion, and never originated an evil suggestion ... and that thus, though at all points assailable through His flesh, He was in all respects holy; seeing wickedness consisteth not in being tempted, but in yielding to the temptation.'[5] Irving believed implicitly in 'the birth-holiness of our Lord Jesus Christ'[6] and stated unambiguously that 'He differed from all men in this respect, that He never sinned'.[7] He was 'a holy thing from the beginning of His creature being',[8] living a sinless life in sinful flesh.[9] It is clear from such statements that the charges brought against Irving were based on *inferences* from what he had said: inferences that he himself had not drawn and could not have drawn.

Thirdly, Irving used extremely provocative language. One worshipper complained of hearing him refer to the humanity of Christ as 'that sinful substance'.[10] In a subsequent conversation Irving was challenged as to whether he believed that Christ, like Paul, had 'the law of sin' in his members, bringing him into captivity. 'Not into captivity,' Irving replied; 'but Christ experienced everything the same as Paul did, except the "captivity".'[11]

His published statements were almost equally bold. God's scheme of redemption, he wrote, was that the Son of God 'should join Himself unto the fallen creation, after it had fallen, and become obnoxious to all the powers of sin and infirmity and rebellion'.[12] Irving clearly meant by this that the Lord's own humanity was capable of sin and rebellion: 'the flesh of Christ, like my flesh, was in its proper nature mortal and corruptible.'[13] The fact that this corruption did not erupt in actual sin was due entirely to the work of the Holy Spirit, by which he was 'prevented from yielding to any of those temptations to which it was brought conscious, and did reject them every one – yea, did mourn and grieve, and pray to God continually, that it might be delivered from the mortality, corruption, temptation which it felt in its fleshly tabernacle'.[14] 'I hold,' he wrote, 'that wherever flesh is mentioned in Scripture, mortality and corruption are the attributes of it; and that when it is said that Christ came in the flesh, it is distinctly averred that He came in a mortal and corruptible substance.'[15] The responsibility of the Holy Spirit was to make this flesh incorruptible: 'I have the Holy Ghost manifested in subduing, restraining, conquering the evil propensities of the fallen manhood, and making it an apt organ for expressing the will of the Father.'[16]

In his later treatise, *On the Human Nature of Christ*, Irving tried to explain what he meant 'whenever I attribute sinful properties and dispositions and inclinations to our Lord's human nature'.[17] The attempt was hardly a success. It involved a sharp separation between the Lord's human nature and his divine person, seemed to leave him in the same position as 'any other' regenerate man and left the reader with the strong impression that Irving's main concern was to insist that the nature which Christ took was, like our own, 'full of sin, and death, and rebellion, and dishonour unto God'.[18] As far as Irving was concerned, what Christ received at conception was 'a regenerate life ... in kind the same which we receive in regeneration, but in measure greater, because of His perfect faith'.[19] He continued: 'This is the substance of our argument: that His human nature was holy in the only way in which holiness under the fall exists or can exist, is spoken of or can be spoken of in Scripture, namely, through inworking or energising of the Holy Ghost ... enforcing His human nature, inclining it, uniting it to God'.[20] It is hardly surprising that such sentiments gave offence.

The early response to Irving was almost entirely critical. Marcus Dods ignored Irving's protestations of belief in the sinlessness of Jesus and accused him of Manicheism, Nestorianism and logical confusion. 'The question is,' Dods concluded, 'can this term ("sinful"), be its meaning what it may, be applied to the flesh of Christ, while it cannot be applied to Christ himself, or to God? While you say that the flesh of Christ was sinful, do you say also that Christ himself was sinful, or that God was sinful?'[21] A. B. Bruce pointed out the antecedents of Irving's teaching in the Spanish adoptionists of the eighth century and the preaching of Gottfried Menken of Bremen in the nineteenth (although there is no evidence that Irving had any direct contact with either of these sources). Bruce further charged Irving with rhetorical inexactitude, accused him of confusing sinless infirmities with vices, and subjected his view of temptation to a rigorous critique, pointing out, among other things, that temptation can come not only from lust but from its opposite – for example, from a holy shrinking from desertion by God: 'Temptations arising out of sinful infirmities may be far fiercer than those which arise out of sinful appetites.' [22]

It was left to Karl Barth to bring Irving in from the cold. In his *Church Dogmatics*, Barth enthusiastically espoused the idea that Christ took a fallen humanity, taking this to mean a corrupt nature (*natura vitiata*), obnoxious to sin and existing in a vile and abject condition. 'There must,' he wrote, 'be no weakening or obscuring of the saving truth that the nature which God assumed in Christ is identical with our own nature as we see it in the light of the Fall. If it were otherwise, how could Christ really be like us? What concern could we have with Him? We stand before God characterised by the Fall. God's Son not only assumed our nature but He entered the concrete form of our nature, under which we stand before God as men damned and lost.'[23] Like Irving, however, Barth denied that this meant actual sin on the Lord's part: 'He was not a sinful man. But inwardly and outwardly His situation was that of a sinful man. He did nothing that Adam did. But He lived life in the form it must take on the basis and assumption of Adam's act.' [24]

Barth, however, had no first-hand acquaintance with Irving's work. He knew of it only through H.R. Mackintosh's *The Person of Jesus Christ*. (Barth met Mackintosh in the summer of 1930, 'on Edinburgh station, where I was waiting for my train to London.... His personality made an unforgettable impression on me: the penetrating thorough-ness ... with which he struggled over the positions of nineteenth-century theology in the light of the Calvinistic traditions of Scotland which were still as alive as ever in him.'[25])

H. R. Mackintosh

Mackintosh's own work is a magisterial survey of the biblical evidence and of post-biblical Christological discussion. Today, it is most notable for its sympathetic treatment of Kenoticism. Mackintosh distanced himself, however, from the earlier forms of this theory advocated by such scholars as Thomasius (*Christi Person und Werk*, 1853) and Gess (*Christi Person und Werk*, 1870-87) and identified more closely with the work of his fellow Scots, D.W. Forrest (*The Authority of Christ*, Edinburgh, 1906) and P.T. Forsyth (*Person and Place of Jesus Christ*, London, 1909).

What particularly attracted Mackintosh was the religious value of *kenosis*: 'It is a conception of immense religious significance. Somehow – to describe the method exactly may of course be beyond us – somehow God in Christ has brought His greatness down to the narrow measures of our life, becoming poor for our sake.... Descending into poverty, shame and weakness, the Lord was stripped of all credit, despoiled of every right, humbled to the very depths of social and historical ignominy, that in this self-abasement of God there might be found the redemption of man.'[26]

The main features of Mackintosh's *kenoticism* are as follows.

First, he insisted on the need to ethicise our concept of God, particularly our concept of immutability. Mackintosh feared that the idea of the changelessness of the Absolute could be – and often was – used to put the very idea of divine self-limitation out

of court. 'Now it is not at all excessive,' he wrote, 'to say that
what Christ reveals in God is rather the infinite mobility of absolute
grace bent on the redemption of the lost, the willingness to do and
bear whatever is compatible with a moral nature. What is
immutable in God is the holy love which makes His essence. We
must let Infinitude be genuinely infinite in its moral expedients;
we must credit God with infinite sacrifice based on His self-
consciousness of omnipotence.'[27] 'Love with resource like God's,'
he continued, 'has a boundless capacity of self-determination. For
us men and our salvation, it may well be, He committed Himself,
in one aspect of his personal being, to a grade of experience
qualified by change and development, thus stooping to conquer
and permitting the conditions of manhood to prevail over His own
freedom. If the alternatives are an unethical conception of
immutability and a pure thought of moral omnipotence, which
makes room for Divine sacrifice, the Christian mind need not
hesitate.'[28]

Secondly, Mackintosh repudiated the notion (proposed by
Thomasius) that *kenosis* consisted in Christ's laying aside the
relative attributes of deity, such as omnipresence and omniscience,
while retaining such *essential* attributes as holiness and love. 'The
distinction is not one which can be maintained,' he wrote: '...to
talk of the abandonment of this or that attribute on the part of the
Eternal Son is a conception too sharp and crude, too rough in
shading, for our present problem. God ceases to be God not merely
when (as with Gess) there is a self-renunciation actually of the
divine consciousness, but even when such qualities as omnipotence
are parted with.'[29]

Thirdly, he suggested that although the divine attributes of the
Son were not laid aside they were modified ('transposed') 'to
function in new ways, to assume new forms of activity',[30] in
accordance with the new condition of the Subject. 'It is possible
to conceive the Son,' Mackintosh wrote, 'who has entered at love's
behest on the region of growth and progress, as now possessing
all the qualities of Godhead in the form of concentrated potency
rather than of full actuality.'[31] This applied particularly to
omniscience, omnipotence and omnipresence. Christ had divine

knowledge within reach, though he took only what was essential to his vocation: 'Though on many subjects He shared the ignorance as well as the knowledge of His contemporaries, yet He had at command all higher truth which can be assimilated by perfect human faculty.'[32] The same was true with regard to power. God may will, for the sake of his human children, to limit his almightiness, translating it into a form compatible with our experience, 'but in the historic Jesus there is a derived power over the souls of men, as over nature, which may be viewed as a modified form of the power of the Godhead.'[33] Omnipresence, Mackintosh admitted, is more baffling. But only at first sight. A transcending of spatial relationships is present and implicit in Christ's redemptive mission – 'in His triumphant capacity, that is, to accomplish in Palestine a universally and eternally valid work unhampered by the bounds of "here and there". As part of history, His work has a date and place, yet its power far transcends them.'[34]

Fourthly, Mackintosh asserted that the life which Jesus lived as a result of 'this divine act of self-abnegation' was 'a life wholly restrained within the bounds of manhood. Outside the conditions imposed by the choice of life as man the Son has no activity or knowledge.'[35] This involved the possibility that 'His primary descent into the sphere of finitude had veiled in nescience His eternal relationship to the Father'.[36] Pursuing this theme, Mackintosh suggested that 'It can only have been in mature manhood and perhaps intermittently that Christ became aware of His divinity – which must have remained for Him an object of *faith* to the very end.'[37] He even seems to limit this awareness of divine sonship to 'high moments of visitation' in the Lord's experience.

This is the weakest link in Mackintosh's exposition. True though it is that Christ would have become aware of his divine identity only gradually, it is unwarranted to delay that self-understanding to 'mature manhood'. In fact, Luke clearly suggests that at a comparatively early age Jesus saw God as 'Abba' (Luke 2:49). It is also unwarranted to say that this self-understanding was 'intermittent'; and even more so to suggest that it was confined to moments of high visitation. So far as we know, the only point at which the sense of divine sonship was eclipsed was on the cross, at the moment of Dereliction (Mark 15:34); and even then the eclipse was only momentary and partial. In fact, the idea that the earthly life was merely human (as distinct from *really* human) would have calamitous consequences for Christian theology. How could something merely human be the supreme – if not quite the only – revelation of God? How could one merely human say, 'He who has seen me has seen the Father' (John 14:9)? And how could one with no consistent sense of divine identity designate himself by titles (such as *Son of God* and *Son of Man*) which clearly imply deity and pre-existence? At this point Mackintosh has no defence against the objection that *Kenoticism*, by definition, deprives us of the right to say that we find God in Jesus.

It may be that Mackintosh himself felt the force of such difficulties. At least, it is very interesting that there are no traces of *Kenoticism* in his later work. The idea is not mentioned at all in *The Christian Experience of Forgiveness* (London, 1927); nor are the kenotic theologians discussed in his last work, *Types of Modern Theology* (Welwyn, 1937). He also appears to have dropped all reference to the Kenotic Theory from his later class lectures.[38]

Donald Baillie

Mackintosh's younger contemporary, Donald Baillie, published his *God Was in Christ* in 1948. Baillie gave an enthusiastic welcome to what he called 'the End of Docetism': 'It may safely be said that practically all schools of theological thought today take the full humanity of our Lord more seriously than has ever been done before by Christian theologians.' He also recognised, however, that not all the results of twentieth century scholarship had been positive. In particular, he was critical of the historical radicalism of such men as Rudolf Bultmann and H. R. Lightfoot: 'I cannot believe that there is any good reason for the defeatism of those who give up all hope of penetrating the tradition and reaching an assured knowledge of the historical personality of Jesus.'[40]

Baillie devoted a substantial portion of his essay (pp. 85-105) to *A Critique of Christologies*. This included a brilliant analysis of the Kenotic Theory, in which he argued that it had no answer to William Temple's question,[41] What was happening to the rest of the universe during the period of our Lord's life? Was the world let loose from the control of the creative Word during the period of his depotentiation? He also argued that Kenoticism implied a theophany rather than an incarnation; and that it seemed to leave no room at all for the traditional doctrine of the *permanence* of the manhood of Christ ('when the days of His flesh come to an end, Christ resumes His divine attributes and His *kenosis*, His humanity, comes to an end'.[42]

Baillie was even more critical of the idea of *anhypostasia* (the notion that the Lord's human nature was impersonal). In this he was following H.R. Mackintosh and R.C. Moberley (*Atonement and Personality*, London, 1901, p. 92). It is not entirely clear, however, what Baillie was objecting to. Few would deny that Jesus was 'a man among men';[43] or that he was an individual man; or even that he had a human centre of consciousness. The question is whether he had a human centre of *self*-consciousness. If so, did he have this as well as a divine centre of self-consciousness, and therefore two selves? True though it is that the man Christ Jesus was an individual over against other men, his human nature did not have an individual existence over against his divine nature. Baillie was sympathetic to the idea of *enhypostasia*, first proposed by Leontius of Byzantium and John of Damascus and reintroduced to English-speaking theology by H.M. Relton.[44] He was not, however, quite convinced. Yet *enhypostasia* (literally, *in*-personal) seems to meet all the difficulties. The humanity of Christ never lacked individuality or personhood. From the very first moment of its existence it was the humanity of the Son of God and as such personalised in him. Yet he, and not merely his human nature (or his divine, for that matter), was the subject of all his acts and experiences.

Baillie's own Christology was rooted firmly in the Nicene tradition, insisting that 'it is impossible to do justice to the incarnation without speaking of it as the coming into history of the eternally pre-existent Son of God'.[45] His most distinctive contribution was his attempt to present the incarnation as a reflection of the paradox of grace (the good actions of a Christian are fully his own actions, yet whatever good there is in our lives is 'all of God'). 'This paradox,' he wrote, 'in its fragmentary form in our own Christian lives is a reflection of that perfect union of God and man in the Incarnation on which our whole Christian life depends, and may therefore be our best clue to the understanding of it.'[46] This is certainly worth exploring,[47] although the obedience of a Christian is due rather to the indwelling of the Spirit than to a union of natures. But Baillie surely comes close to both Nestorianism and Adoptionism when he suggests that the incarnation of the divine Word in Christ was conditioned by his own continual response. It is indeed true that moment by moment Christ was choosing humiliation and adhering to *kenosis*. But it cannot be true that moment by moment he was choosing to be incarnate. The Gospels record his being tempted to abandon the path of service but we have no record of any temptation to go back on the Enfleshment. It is also misleading to suggest that 'when at last God broke through into human life with full revelation and became incarnate, must we not say that in a sense it was because here at last a man was perfectly receptive?'[48] The man did not exist prior to the incarnation.

James Denney

Mackintosh and Baillie were discussing the traditional doctrinal issues associated with Christology. James Denney's *Jesus and the Gospel* did something completely different. It looked at the questions raised by the radically critical approach to Christian origins and the resultant 'quest of the historical Jesus'. J.G. Machen, in the course of arguing that 'Jesus most certainly did not keep His Person out of His gospel, but on the contrary presented Himself as the Saviour of men' commended Denney warmly: 'The demonstration of that fact was the highest merit of the late James Denney ... Denney has shown that no matter what view be taken of the sources underlying the Gospels, and no matter what elements in the Gospels be rejected as secondary, still even the supposed "historical Jesus," as He is left after the critical process is done, plainly presented Himself, not merely as an example for faith, but as the object of faith.'[49]

The tribute was well merited. *Jesus and the Gospel* is a superb essay in historical apologetics, rivalled only by Hoskyns and Davey's widely acclaimed classic, *The Riddle of the New Testament*.[50]

The background to Denney's study was the dictum of Adolph Harnack: 'The Gospel, as Jesus proclaimed it, has to do with the Father only and not with the Son.'[51] The role of Messiah, according to Harnack, was merely to lead men to God and he did this by serving as an example and inspiration: 'Fire is kindled only by fire; personal life only by personal forces ... history shows that he is the one who brings the weary and the heavy laden to God; and, again, that he it was who raised mankind to the new level; and his teaching is still the touchstone, in that it brings men to bliss and brings them to judgement.'[52] Jesus, Harnack insisted, was no part of his own creed: 'even when he says, "Whosoever shall confess me before men, him will I confess also before my Father which is in heaven," he is thinking of people *doing as he did*; he means the confession which shows itself in feeling and action. How great a departure from what he thought and enjoined is involved in putting a "Christological" creed in the forefront of the Gospel, and in teaching that before a man can approach it he must learn to think rightly about Christ.'[53]

Denney made two responses to this.

First, he argued that Jesus occupied exactly the same place in the New Testament church as he did in historical Christianity: 'There is no Christianity known to the New Testament except that in which He has a place all His own, a place of absolute significance, to which there is no analogy elsewhere.'[54] Denney supported his thesis by carefully examining all the layers of the New Testament tradition, from the earliest Christian preaching to the Gospel of John.

Secondly, Denney argued, almost to the point of overkill, that the Christian attitude to Jesus went back to his own self-consciousness. he himself, as recorded in history, justifies the Christian religion as it is exhibited in the New Testament:[55] 'When

we look back from the Christian religion as the New Testament
exhibits it, and as it is still exhibited in the Christian church, to
the historical Jesus, we see a Person, who is not only equal to the
place which Christian faith assigns him, but who assumes that
place naturally and spontaneously as his own.'[56]

In arguing his case Denney scrupulously refrained from using
any evidence which the sceptical might deem suspect. For example,
he refused to argue from the title *Son of God* in Mark 1:1 (because
the text is uncertain); he laid little stress on the resurrection
narratives ('the least important part of the evidence') or on the
empty tomb; and he virtually ignored the Gospel of John (which
'could only be used inconclusively in the present discussion').

On the other hand, he made some telling criticisms of the
techniques used in historical criticism of the Gospels. For example,
he took issue with the principle of non-intentionality, which
Schmiedel hád defined as follows in *Encyclopaedia Biblica*:
'When a profane historian finds before him a historical document
which testifies to the worship of a hero unknown to other sources,
he attaches first and foremost importance to those features which
cannot be deduced merely from the fact of this worship, and he
does so on the simple and sufficient ground that they would not
be found in this source unless the author had met with them as
fixed data of tradition. The same fundamental principle may safely
be applied in the case of the gospels, for they also are all of them
written by worshippers of Jesus.'[57] Denney commented acidly:
'We only put this more simply when we say that anything in the
gospels may be regarded as signally true if it is inconsistent with
the worship of Jesus.'[58] Instead, he said, 'It is not doing anything
but justice to the whole of the fact involved if we say that we
ought to have a bias in favour of what connects Christianity with
Jesus, rather than in favour of ideas which fix a great gulf between
them.'[59] Jesus must have been great enough to account for the
phenomenon he created. And Denney went on to show that he
was, engaging in a massive induction of evidence, with particular
stress on the self-revelation of Jesus. The place given to him in
Christianity is given to him only because he claimed it as his own.

In his conclusion, Denney extended the scope of the discussion, venturing into wider practical and principial issues.

For example, he challenged those who alleged that religion should not be entangled in historical investigations. In this connection, he faced up squarely to Lessing's famous dictum, 'The accidental truths of history can never become the proof of necessary truths of reason.'[60] 'Christianity,' Denney retorted, 'does not mean the recognition of necessary truths of reason, but an attitude of the soul to God, determined by Christ; and history is not to the religious man a chapter of accidents, but the stage on which a divine purpose is achieved which could not be more ineptly described than by calling it accidental.'[61] As such, it can disclose something of eternal truth. Historical realities like the Personality, the Self-consciousness, the Resurrection and the growing Ascendancy of Jesus were anything but 'contingent historical truths': 'whatever we mean when we speak of divine necessity may be predicated of all.'[62] They were indeed rooted in the past, but they had 'divine meaning' and present relevance. In Christ the historical became eternal.

Denney also took up the claim that 'the historical Jesus is irrecoverably lost to us; we do not know what He was, we only know how those who believed in Him represented Him to their own minds'.[63] Denney questioned the assumptions behind this conclusion, the primary one being that Jesus was exactly what other men were. If this assumption were correct, then, of course, the Gospels represent an idealising of Jesus, 'representing Him in history as acting in the role which He fills in Christian faith.'[64] This means, said Denney, that anything in the Gospels which positively connects Jesus with Christianity is 'idealising': a creation of the believing community. Such an assumption is ridiculous. There must have been something in Jesus to account for the church's 'idealising' of him and for the religion he generated. 'To admit this, however, is to admit that the Jesus exactly like ourselves who is assumed to stand behind the gospel history, is an illegitimate assumption; if He had been no more than we are, the wonder of the Christian religion and of the New Testament would never have come to be.'[65] Denney concluded: 'He stands alone, not only in the faith of His followers, but in His own apprehension of what He is to God and man.'[66]

The curious thing is that from this platform Denney went on to launch an attack on creeds and credal subscription. There must, he said, be unreserved recognition of the place which Christ has always held in evangelical faith, but there must also be 'entire intellectual freedom in thinking out what this implies'.[67] Soundness in the faith was one thing; soundness in doctrine ('the acceptance of some established intellectual construction of faith') was quite another. Denney lauded the Wesleyans as the only religious society on earth which required nothing of men in order to their admission apart from a desire to save their souls. By contrast, he indulged in unrestrained criticism of existing creeds, particularly the Nicene. For example, comparing Nicea with the Westminster Confession he wrote: 'When a man speaks of giving up the Westminster Confession for the Nicene Creed, one can only think that he has no true appreciation of either. The Westminster Confession contains everything that is in the Nicene Creed, but the writer has no hesitation in saying that this is the least valuable part of what it contains, and that which has least prospect of permanence.'[68] The idea that Christ was *homoousios* with the Father was, in Denney's view a purely metaphysical proposition; very few people knew what the Nicene fathers meant by it; and no one knows whether all who use it now use it in the same sense ('or rather, it is as certain as anything can be that they do not').

It is not entirely clear what lay behind Denney's animus at this point. To some extent it was a concern to formulate the faith in exclusively New Testament language. But his sweeping criticisms of post-biblical creeds showed a curious lack of historical awareness. Arianism and Athanasius, he argued, both gave answers to a question which multitudes of Christians never ask; and one 'may be convinced, as the writer is, that the Arian answer is quite unreal, and as convinced that the Athanasian answer explains nothing'.[69] But the issue raised by Arianism is implicit in all Christianity: Is it right to worship Jesus? And however provisional the answer given by Athanasius he did assert unambiguously the deity of Christ and thus placed Christian practice on a solid foundation.

Even more intriguing is Denney's view of the singularity of the Wesleyan approach to church membership. His conviction that the basis of church membership should be an experience of Christ (faith) rather than credal subscription was absolutely correct. But where in Scotland did he find any practice to the contrary? Presbyterianism has always practised what Denney preached, namely, that all who have faith in Christ are to be welcomed into the church (because, in the highest sense, they already belong to it). It has never been the custom to require subscription to any formula. Even the strictest Scottish traditions have focused on experience ('conversion narrative') rather than on credal orthodoxy. What the Scottish churches did insist on, of course, was that all office-bearers subscribe to the Confession of Faith. But this is a separate issue, raising quite different questions. Suffice for the moment to suggest that there is at least a *prima facie* wisdom in expecting more of a shepherd than of a sheep.

What is especially fascinating, however, is the form of words which Denney himself proposed as the symbol of the church's unity: 'I believe in God through Jesus Christ His only Son, our Lord and Saviour.'

The striking thing here is Denney's omitting to call Jesus *God*. It was no accident. As his aversion to Athanasius and the Nicene Creed suggested, this was an area where he had real difficulties and even during his life-time his hesitation gave concern to his friends, particularly William Robertson Nicoll. In a letter of 4 December, 1908, Nicoll complimented Denney on *Jesus and the Gospel*: 'It seems to me in the main a most powerful, convincing and timely argument.'[70] But he went on to say: 'I kept on reading in search of an unequivocal statement that Jesus is God. Very likely I have missed it, but I did not find it. There are Trinitarians, Binitarians, Arians and Unitarians. You repudiate Arianism and Unitarianism, but I have the impression that you would not repudiate Binitarianism.'

Denney replied as follows: 'as for your remark that you missed an unequivocal statement that Jesus is God, I feel inclined to say that such a statement seems unattractive to me just because it is impossible to make it unequivocal. It is not the true way to say a true thing. I think I have made it plain that for me to worship Jesus as God is worshipped, to trust Him as God is trusted, to owe to Him what we can owe to God alone, is the essence of Christianity. I have said in so many words that no one means what a Christian means by God, unless he includes in that all that a Christian means by "Father, Son and Spirit". This I hold to be the Catholic doctrine of the Trinity, but I dread ways of putting it which do nothing but challenge contradiction. "Jesus is God" seems to me one of those provocative ways, and therefore I avoid it. It has the same objectionableness in my mind as calling Mary the Mother of God.'[71]

In a further letter Nicoll referred to the English Arians of the eighteenth century (among whom he included Watts and Doddridge) and added, 'the Arians of that time would, I think, have gone as far as you do now – at least some of them would.'[72] Denney replied that he did not think there was any difference between himself and Nicoll on this issue: 'When you say that you do from your heart believe that God was manifest in the flesh, I am sure I can say the same.... Probably the aversion I have to such an expression as "Jesus is God" is linguistic as much as theological.... It is because God is to all intents a proper noun with us, which, if it is used as a predicate at all, must make an equation with the subject (Jesus is God being the same thing as Jesus = God), that it seems not only to me, but I am sure to most people, an unnatural way of declaring their faith in Christ as Immanuel – God with us. Jesus is man as well as God, in some way therefore both less and more than God; and consequently a form of proposition which in our idiom suggests inevitably the precise equivalence of Jesus and God does some kind of injustice to the truth.'[73]

Nicoll's concern was shared by his friend H.R. Mackintosh, who wrote, 'He [Denney] appears to have embarked on the perilous and fateful task of finding a mean between Trinitarianism and Arianism.'[74] Mackintosh referred to a conversation he had with Dr Alexander Maclaren of Manchester ('who has a keener insight into the New Testament than anyone else I know'), who 'agreed with me that Denney's formula is a formula for the admission of

Arians and Unitarians. All Arians would sign it gladly, and much more. Maclaren, who, knew James Martineau very intimately, said that James Martineau would have jumped to sign it.' Mackintosh concluded: 'I have written again to Denney, but I am in perplexity about the book. There is a singular vein of scepticism in him, for all his apparent orthodoxy.'

It is interesting to look at references to this subject in Denney's other works. In his commentary *The Epistles to the Thessalonians*[75] (*The Expositor's Bible*, London, 1892), he offers no comment on 2 Thessalonians 1:12, which in the opinion of a considerable body of scholarship (including Rudolf Bultmann[76]) should be translated, 'according to the grace of our God and Lord, Jesus Christ' (NIV mg.). This rendering is improbable, but the significant thing is that Denney shows no interest. In his exposition of Second Corinthians in the same series he makes a tantalising comment on 2 Corinthians 5:19: 'It is safe to say that "God was in Christ" is a sentence which neither St Paul nor any other New Testament writer could have conceived.' Unfortunately, he does not amplify. He is correct to dismiss the KJV rendering. But if we cannot say that Christ was God or that God was in Christ, what can we say?

It was probably inevitable that when it fell to him to comment on Romans 9:5 Denney would argue against the view that the designation *God* in this passage refers to Christ: 'I agree with those who would put a colon or a period after *sarka*, and make the words that follow refer not to Christ but to the Father.'[77] This would give the rendering: 'to them belong the patriarchs, and of their race, according to the flesh, is the Christ. God who is over all be blessed for ever. Amen' (RSV). In support of this interpretation Denney relied heavily on the argument of Meyer to the effect that Paul never used the word *theos* of Christ, because he preferred popular, concrete, monotheistic language (by contrast with John, who preferred the metaphysical language of Alexandria). How far we are justified in speaking so confidently of the inner workings of the apostolic mind is a moot point, but Denney had no doubts: 'If we ask ourselves point blank, whether Paul, as we know his mind from his epistles, would express his sense of Christ's greatness by calling him God blessed for ever, it seems to me almost impossible to answer in the affirmative. Such an assertion is not on the same plane with the conception of Christ which meets us everywhere in the Apostle's writings.'[78] All one can say is that many who have asked the same question have come up with the opposite answer.

The closest Denney came to a formal deliverance on Christology was in *Studies in Theology*.[79] But even here the same hesitation is apparent. Denney alludes to, but does not discuss, John's statement that the Word was God (John 1:1). He declares his belief that he was God's Son in a unique sense, that he was the definitive revelation of God, that he was pre-existent and that his life on earth represented a genuine incarnation of God. He repudiated the humanitarian Christ of Ritschl and the depotentiated Christ of Kenoticism. But he did not say: Jesus (or Christ) is God.

James Denney was a careful, thoughtful and erudite scholar and his position on this question is not as baffling as might appear at first sight. The problem that perplexed him is already implicit in the language of John's prologue: 'the Word was God.' John deliberately avoids the definite article. The Word was *theos* but he was not *ho theos*. The reasons for this were not only grammatical (that predicative nouns following the verb *to be* normally lack the definite article) but theological. To have described Christ as *ho theos* would have meant either that he is the Father (which he is not) or that he is the exhaustive totality of God (which again he is not). God, designated exhaustively, is 'the Father and the Son and the Holy Spirit'. Even so conservative an exegete as B.F. Westcott, who had no reservations about calling Jesus *God* could write: 'It would be pure Sabellianism to say "the Word was *ho theos*".'[80]

On the other hand there is little doubt that Denney (who did not use John 1:1 as part of his argument) carried his scruples too far. It is impossible to express in English the distinction between *theos* and *ho theos*, unless with Moffat we resort to the use of an adjective ('the Logos was divine') or with the New English Bible to circumlocution ('what God was, the word was'). Furthermore, in English the statement 'the Word was God' does not carry heretical connotations, although it does always require clarification to avoid the risk of Patripassianism and Sabellianism. Above all, Denney ignored the fact that the New Testament itself explicitly calls Jesus *God* (see, for example, John 1:1; 1:18; 20:28, Romans 9:5; Titus 2:13; Hebrews 1:8 and 2 Peter 1:1). The interpretation of each of these passages is, inevitably, disputed, but it is impossible to ignore their cumulative force (especially since the standard argument against each of them is that the New Testament *never* calls Jesus *God*). It is also quite impossible to explain later Christian usage without some clear mandate from the New Testament. For example, Ignatius, as Bultmann points out, 'speaks of Christ as God as if it were a thing to be taken quite for granted'. There is a typical instance in his *Epistle to the Ephesians*: 'For our God, Jesus the Christ, was conceived in the womb by Mary.' The Fathers were hardly likely to initiate such a revolutionary practice without the sanction of the apostles themselves.

The real question, however, is to what extent Denney himself had reservations which went beyond considerations of grammar and verbal precision. Was he a temperamental sceptic? Or was it mere iconoclasm, born of an impatience with tradition? It is impossible to answer. But if H.R. Mackintosh was correct (and we have no reason to doubt him) that Denney did not believe in the existence of the Devil or in the Second Advent,[81] it would hardly be surprising, in these circumstances, if he had real, as well as academic, doubts about the *homoousion*.

Which, as he himself would have been quick to point out, is not the same as saying that we should doubt his personal relationship with the Saviour.

T. F. Torrance

T.F. Torrance was a student of H.R. Mackintosh's but seems to have imbibed little of his mentor's interest in *kenosis*. The real influences on his thought have been Macleod Campbell, Edward Irving and Karl Barth. The Fathers and Reformers whom Torrance cites copiously are read through the eyes of these later thinkers.

Torrance lays great stress on the *homoousion*, the 'king-pin of the Nicene-Constantinopolitan Creed'. The word itself is not sacrosanct, he admits, but the idea it encapsulates is absolutely vital to Christianity. Otherwise, what happens in Christ has nothing to do with any *self*-giving or *self*-revealing on the part of the eternal God.[82] Jesus' acts are saving acts precisely because they are divine acts. If the *homoousion* is not true the cross is unintelligible, but if it is true then 'Jesus Christ, even in the midst of our death which he made his own, even in the midst of our betrayal of him, is the Word and Hand of God stretched out to save us, the very heart of God Almighty beating with the pulse of his infinite love within the depth of our lost humanity in order to vanquish and do away with everything that separates man from God'.[83]

The *homoousion*, according to Torrance, is also of profound epistemological significance, because it means that the Father/ Son and Son/Father relationship 'falls within the very being of God'.[84] It follows from this that we can be confident that what God is to us in Jesus he is in himself: the economic and the ontological trinity are one and the same.[85] 'There is no God,' Torrance had written earlier, 'except He who has shown us His face in Jesus Christ, so that we cannot go behind the back of Christ to find God, or know anything about Him apart from this God, for there is no other God than this God.'[86]

Torrance's enthusiasm for the *homoousion* is paralleled by his aversion to Apollinarianism. This is set out particularly in his essay, 'The Mind of Christ in Worship: The Problem of Apollinarianism in the Liturgy'.[87] Torrance warmly endorses Athanasius' insistence that when we think of the Son becoming flesh 'we must include under that term all our human affections proper to human nature, including weakness, anxiety, agitation, passion, ignorance as well as the sentient characteristics of human beings, for the purpose of the economic condescension was to renew the whole man, not least his *mind*, in Christ'.[88] He is equally enthusiastic about Cyril of Alexandria: 'Cyril considered it of the utmost importance that in his complete oneness with us Christ plumbed the depths of our most intense human experiences, so that from the depths he might engage in intense supplication and prayer to the Father, not only as an example for us to follow, important as that is for all our worship, but as the model of his vicarious mediation on our behalf.'[89]

It is not always easy to disentangle the thinking of these Fathers from Torrance's exegetical interpolations. He does, however, make his own thinking plain elsewhere, constantly invoking the principle that 'the unassumed is the unhealed' and pushing the idea that Christ entered into our human mind to its furthest limits. In *The Mediation of Christ*, for example, he declares: 'it is the alienated *mind* of man that God had laid hold of in Jesus Christ in order to redeem it and effect reconciliation deep within the rational centre of human being.'[90] Later he writes to the same effect: 'In Jesus God himself descended to the very bottom of our human existence where we are alienated and antagonistic, into the very hell of our godlessness and despair, laying fast hold of us and taking our cursed condition upon himself, in order to embrace us for ever in his reconciling love.'[91]

In pursuance of this theme Torrance (encouraged, no doubt, by the example of Barth) went on to reintroduce to Scotland the peculiar Christology of Edward Irving: 'the Incarnation is to be understood as the coming of God to take upon himself our fallen human nature, our actual human existence laden with sin and guilt, our humanity diseased in mind and soul in its estrangement or alienation from the Creator.'[92] Torrance claims that such a conclusion is inevitable if we take seriously Paul's statement in Romans 8:3 that God sent his Son 'in the likeness of flesh of sin'. He also claims that the idea that Christ took our fallen humanity, including our depraved mind, prevailed generally among the Greek Fathers. This is extremely doubtful. Athanasius frequently speaks of Christ assuming flesh but (notwithstanding the impression created by Torrance,[93]) he never asserts that that meant Christ assuming our corruption and sinfulness. In fact, some modern patristic scholars have doubted whether Athanasius had anything like an adequate doctrine of the incarnation at all. Harnack accused him of erasing from his Christology 'almost every trait which recalls the historical Jesus of Nazareth';[94] and R.P.C Hanson concluded 'that whatever else the *Logos* incarnate is in Athanasius' account of him, he is not a human being'.[95] It is even possible that Apollinarianism was a direct result of defects in Athanasius' thought. As G.L. Prestige pointed out, he was so thoroughly preoccupied with the thought of God in Christ reconciling the world to Himself that he retained little interest in Christ as a distinctive human being and disregarded the importance of his human consciousness".[96] All this seems light-years away from the Athanasius of T.F. Torrance.

Equally, true though it is that such Fathers as Gregory of Nazianzus constantly affirmed that 'what Christ has not assumed he has not healed' they never meant by this that Christ took fallen human nature. For the purposes of the Apollinarian controversy the 'unassumed' was not fallenness but the human mind of Christ. From this point of view the most ardent of Irving's opponents would have endorsed the principle that the unassumed is the unhealed, insisting that Christ took not simply a true human body but a reasonable human soul (*anima rationalis*). They would not have conceded, however, that a reasonable human soul was necessarily a fallen one; nor that it would in any way have furthered the work of redemption for Christ to have taken our corruption as well as our guilt.

There are three major objections to this Irving-Torrance theory.

First, it does not pay sufficient attention to the extreme care with which Paul chooses his words in Romans 8:3. He does not say that Christ took sinful flesh (or flesh of sin). He says only that he took the *likeness* of sinful flesh. Calvin goes as far as is safe: 'he saith that Christ came *in the similitude of sinful flesh*, because, albeit the flesh of Christ was stained with no blots, yet to the sight it seemed sinful, so far forth as he sustained that punishment which was due to our sins.'[97] Karl Barth's gloss *sin-controlled flesh*[98] is totally unwarrantable. In fact, far from asserting unambiguously that Christ took fallen human nature, this passage, in the judgement of some modern scholars, is docetic. John Knox, for example, writes: 'When this passage is considered in connection with the most natural meaning of Philippians 2:7-8, I believe we have to recognise the presence in Paul's thought, at least sometimes or in some connections, of a reservation, or misgiving, as to the full genuineness of the humanity of Jesus.'[99]

Secondly, the Irving-Torrance theory has no answer to the charge of Nestorianism. If Christ had a fallen human nature does that mean that he, a divine person, was fallen? If not, was there another (human) person who was fallen? Irving was to some extent aware of this problem and attempted to extricate himself by detaching the human nature from the person. The nature was sinful, the person was holy.[100] But this is only a restatement of the problem, not a solution.

Thirdly, the theory fails to take account of the historical meaning of *fallen*. A fallen person is one who has lost his original righteousness and become corrupt in his whole nature ('totally depraved'). This is what Christ came to save us from. It is certainly not what he was.

Torrance also shares with Irving a commitment to some form of the idea of incarnational redemption. He insists time and again that Christ sanctified the whole of human nature in the very act of assuming it. This idea occurs in such early works as *The School of Faith*, where Torrance speaks of the incarnational union as dealing with our original sin, 'or as sanctifying our fallen human nature through bringing it into healing and sanctifying union with holy divine nature.'[101] The same idea occurs in *Theology in Reconstruction*: 'In this union he both assumed our fallen human nature, taking it from the Virgin Mary, and sanctified it in the very act of assumption and all through his holy Life he lived in it from the beginning to the end. Thus our redemption begins from his very birth, so that we must regard the Incarnation, even in its narrower sense, as redeeming even, reaching out to its full *telos* in the death and resurrection.'[102] In *The Mediation of Christ* he even goes so far as to say that Jesus Christ 'healed the ontological split in human being through the hypostatic and atoning union which he embodied within it'.[103]

According to Torrance there are respectable historical precedents for this view. He attributes it, for example, to Robert Bruce: 'If Bruce thought of the satisfaction of Christ as freeing us from our actual sins, it is clear that he thought of His perfect purity in incarnation and birth as covering our original sin, or as sanctifying our human nature. This stress upon incarnational redemption in Christ Bruce sandwiched in between his accounts of Christ's active and passive obedience, for it belongs to the very heart of His saving work.'[104] Torrance claims, too, the support of the Fathers, particularly of Athanasius: 'Thus for Athanasius the act of assuming our flesh of sin and corruption was *at the same time* a healing and hallowing of our human nature in Christ.'[105]

Irving, too, held to a theory of incarnational redemption. One of the central concerns of *The Doctrine of the Incarnation Opened* was to 'open ... how God, by uniting the person of His Son to fallen flesh, doth thereby reconcile the whole lump of fallen humanity unto Himself, and is enabled, through Christ, to save as many as it pleaseth Him'.[106] But he would not have been happy with Torrance's way of expressing things. Irving completely repudiated the idea that the human nature of Christ was sanctified from birth by the power of the Holy Spirit. He makes this clear in the Preface to his treatise *On the Human Nature of Christ* where, having stated that the work which Christ did was to reconcile, sanctify, quicken and glorify this human nature of ours which is full of sin and death and rebellion, he continues: 'The most part of those who are opposed to the truth agree in this; but differ from us in maintaining that the substance of human nature underwent a change in the miraculous conception. We maintain that it underwent no change, but was full of fellowship and community with us all His life long, and was not changed but by the resurrection.'[107] Earlier, in his *Sermons on the Incarnation*, he had written to the same effect: 'With humility be it spoken, but yet with truth and verity, that the fallen humanity could not have been sanctified and redeemed by the union of the Son alone; which directly leadeth unto an inmixing and confusion of the Divine with the human nature, that pestilent heresy of Eutyches. The human nature is thoroughly fallen; and without a thorough communication, inhabitation, and empowering of a Divine substance, it cannot again be brought up pure and holy. Such a union leads directly to the apotheosis or deification of the creature, and this again does away with the mystery of a trinity in the Godhead.'[108]

The truth is, as he himself recognised,[109] that Irving's theory required not simply a humanity which was identical with ours in origin but one identical with ours in *life*. The two essentials for which he strove – the temptability of Jesus and his sympathy with his people – both required this. A humanity healed and sanctified in the very act of assumption would have been useless for his purposes because it would have differed from that of believers. As far as Irving was concerned, it was the living, struggling, suffering Jesus who had sinful, fallen flesh.

The problem with all theories of incarnational redemption is that they contradict so flagrantly the New Testament's insistence on the centrality of the cross. This insistence itself scarcely requires proof. Paul expresses it in 1 Corinthians 2:2: 'I decided to know nothing among you except Jesus Christ and him crucified;' and again in Galatians 6:14: 'far be it from me to glory except in the cross of our Lord Jesus Christ.' Jesus himself made plain that the primary reason for his coming into the world was 'to give his life a ransom for many' (Mark 10:45); and when he instituted the central sacrament of Christian worship its symbols, word and actions were all chosen with a view to proclaiming his death (1 Cor. 11:26). In accordance with this the New Testament traces every aspect of atonement back to the death of Christ. For example, we have redemption by his blood (Eph. 1:7); by death he won victory over the powers of death (Heb. 2:14); and his blood is the God-appointed expiation and peace-maker (Rom. 3:25). By contrast, when attention is focused on the incarnation, what is stressed is not atonement but the compassion gained through real human experience: 'he had to be made like his brethren in every respect, so that he might become a merciful and faithful high priest' (Heb. 2:17).

Even those Fathers whom Torrance claims as champions of the idea of incarnational redemption retained this emphasis on the death of Christ as the supreme moment in redemption, sometimes expressing themselves in strikingly Anselmic terms. In his *De Incarnatione*, i, 9, for example, Athanasius wrote: 'And thus taking from our bodies one of like nature, because all were under penalty of the corruption of death He gave it over to death in the stead of all, and offered it to the Father.... Whence, by offering unto death the body He Himself had taken, as an offering and sacrifice free from any stain, straightway He put away death from all His peers by the offering of an equivalent. For being over all, the Word of God naturally by offering His own temple and corporeal instrument for the life of all satisfied the debt by His death.' Only thus (and not by the mere possession of a common nature, although that had its own importance) did He clothe men with incorruption. This is not to say that Athanasius held an Anselmic view of the atonement. But he was certainly no Irvingite.

Of course the idea of union with Christ is prominent in the New Testament, both in the sense of our being in him and in the sense of his being in us. But this is very much more a spiritual union (through the Holy Spirit) than an ontological one (a union of natures). What is decisive is not whether our *nature* is in Christ, but whether we personally are in Christ: the possibility is a very real one that we may be fully human and yet not be in Christ (Eph. 2:12). Besides, the focal point of union-with-Christ passages is very seldom the incarnation but either the cross or the resurrection. We have been crucified with Christ (Gal. 2:20, Rom. 6:6); and we have been raised up together with him (Rom. 6:5, Eph. 2:6). It is not the merely incarnate Christ but the crucified and risen One who is the repository of redemption (Eph. 1:7).

Nor is it permissible to view the cross as a mere extension of the incarnation, stemming organically from the decision to make himself nothing (Phil. 2:7). How then could we account for the agony in the Garden (Luke 22:44) or for the deliberate emphasis of John 13:1 that Jesus consciously proceeded to the cross constrained by his limitless love for his people? Above all, how, if the cross is a mere extension of the incarnation, can we explain the sustained New Testament emphasis on the love of the Father? No theory of incarnational redemption can explain why God did not spare his own Son but delivered him up for us all (Rom. 8:32).

The remaining point in Torrance's Christology is his stress on the vicarious humanity of Christ. For example, Christ is not only the Word of God to man but man's perfect response to that word.[110] He is also the One who vicariously believes; the One who was vicariously sanctified (so that sanctification, no less than justification, is *imputed* to us);[111] and the One in whom we enjoy a vicarious assurance – a subjective justification in which Christ, in our place, trusted in God's love towards us. 'We may summarise this,' writes Torrance, in language clearly reminiscent of Macleod

Campbell, 'by saying that Jesus Christ was not only the fulfilment and embodiment of God's righteous and holy Act or *dikaioma*, but also the embodiment of our act of faith and trust and obedience toward God. He stood in our place, taking our cause upon him, also as Believer, as the Obedient One who was himself justified before God as his beloved Son in whom he was well pleased. He offered to God a perfect confidence and trust, a perfect faith and response which we are unable to offer, and he appropriated all God's blessings which we are unable to appropriate.'[112]

Torrance also applies the idea of the vicarious humanity of Christ to the practice of Christian worship. The argument here is that if we do justice to the fulness of the Lord's humanity then we shall not only worship the Father *through* the Son but *along with* the Son; that is, we shall share in the Son's worship of the Father. 'Christian worship,' writes Torrance, 'is properly a form of the life of Jesus Christ ascending to the Father in the life of those who are so intimately related to him through the Spirit, that when they pray to the Father through Christ, it is Christ the Incarnate Son who honours, worships and glorifies the Father in them.'[113]

At first sight Torrance's exposition of this theme appears to involve a thorough-going Christo-monism in which the work of Christ is everything and that of the believer is insignificant and even needless: we shall be saved regardless of our response because he responded for us. Yet there are so many qualifications built into the exposition that although the initial reaction is one of shock a careful re-reading usually shows that the thinking is much less revolutionary than appears.

What has to be said, first of all, is that this stress on the vicarious humanity of Christ does not accord with the New Testament's portrayal of the distinctive roles of the Son and the Spirit in the work of redemption. The Spirit is not the primary actor in the great drama of atonement; and the Son is not the primary enabler in the life of the believer. So far as worship is concerned, for example, the stress falls firmly on the role of the Holy Spirit. We worship in Spirit and in truth (John 4:23). We sing in the Spirit (1 Cor. 14:15, Eph. 5:19). We pray in the Spirit (1 Cor. 14:15).

Secondly, while the work of the Son is vicarious the work of the Holy Spirit is not. Christ died in our place, but the Spirit does not believe in our place. He enables us to believe, but it is we who believe, just as it is we who repent, worship and mortify sin. All these activities occur by the aid of the Spirit but he does not perform them instead of us.

Thirdly, the term *vicarious* cannot be used unequivocally even in relation to Christ. At one point – the cross – *vicarious* means *substitute*. Christ died in our place: that is, he died so that we should not die. He was a substitutionary-ransom (*antilutron*, 1 Tim. 2:6). In other instances, however, *vicarious* means *representative*; and in yet others it means *solidarity*. When Torrance speaks of the vicarious humanity of Christ (particularly in relation to faith, assurance and worship) he is using the word in this last sense. Yet the impression of originality is due entirely to the fact that the reader instinctively takes it in the first sense. Christ is undoubtedly a believer *with* us (Heb. 12:2). But he is not a believer *instead of* us. He enjoys assurance with us, but he does not enjoy it instead of us. Even more important, while Christ worships with us he does not worship instead of us. In sum, while it is true that because Christ became a curse we shall never be accursed (Gal. 3:13) it is not true that because he believed and worshipped we need not believe and worship.

Older writers
Yet, however stimulating some of these modern Scottish essays in Christology, it is an enormous pity that they have so completely ignored their orthodox predecessors. The older writers may have lacked originality to the extent that they never deviated from Chalcedonian orthodoxy. But they handled that orthodoxy itself with great sensitiveness and creativity. They certainly had no reservations about the humanity of Christ. In fact, the idea of our Lord's identification with men has never been better expressed than it was by Stewart of Cromarty: 'as the tabernacle after all was as truly a tent as the humblest in the camp of Israel, so Christ is as truly man as the meanest of our race. The blood which flows in the veins of the Hottentot, or springs under the lash from the back of an American slave, is that "one" same blood which flows

in the veins of the Son of God.'[114]

Stewart also spoke uninhibitedly of the temptations of Christ. God, he wrote, perilled everything on his Son's absolute infallibility, 'as if He would say, "If He fail, let My throne be overturned, and I Myself cease to be God." The holy Son of God was tempted as if He could commit sin, and as if it were necessary that His principles should be put to the test.'[115] In Stewart's judgement, the Son's deity in no way mitigated the force of the temptations. '"Ah, but," you say, "He was the divine Son of God, there was no fear for Him." We have no reason to think that His deity afforded Him the slightest relief from the pains of hunger. And thus He and all His suffering people are perfectly on a level. By the exercise of His divine power He might not turn the stones into bread. To do so would be sin; and just so is it sinful for you to resort to any unlawful means to supply your wants, even when they arise in the ordinary course of life. "But," you say, "He knew it would soon end, and I know not when relief may come." It does not appear from His answer to Satan that He knew this. His circumstances seem to have been much the same as those of any ordinary man suffering hunger and with nothing to eat. How entirely, then, is His fellow-feeling of infirmity under suffering unbroken by His deity!'[116]

James M'Lagan

This question of the Lord's temptability was also explored by James M'Lagan in *A Sermon on Hebrews IV.15* appended to Dods' *On the Incarnation of the Word*.[117] 'It was not a few kinds only of our earthly struggles, apart from others, that he admitted into his heart,' wrote M'Lagan, 'but he stood successively in all the main flood-gates of tribulation, and there made trial of the worst that mortal man can endure, whether from the hostility of a disordered world, or from the rage of fallen angels, or from the wrath of offended Heaven.'[118] M'Lagan stressed the reality of the resulting temptations. They were more sharp and terrible than those of any other man: 'What though he had no irregular or exaggerated passions to restrain? He had holy, just, pure, heavenly affections, strong in proportion to the greatness of his soul, and warm in proportion to the brightness of dignity of their objects; which he was called upon, by the nature of his undertaking, not only to control, but for a season to thwart so painfully, and to turn aside so violently from their natural courses, that he must have needed to exercise a persevering strength of self-denial altogether matchless; and must have had in his heart experience far beyond what mere mortality could have endured, of the profoundest sorrow, the keenest anguish and the harshest mortification.'[119]

Like Stewart, M'Lagan recoiled from the idea that the fact of his being God cushioned the Lord against temptation. He referred to 'certain ill-defined notions of the share which our Lord's Godhead must have taken in supernaturally sustaining his human powers while under temptation', and went on to say: 'According to the scriptures, then, it was the work of that Divinity which is mysteriously united with manhood in his person, – not to raise his suffering nature to such a height of glorious power as would render all trial slight and contemptible; but to confer upon it such strength as would be infallibly sufficient – I say *infallibly sufficient* – but not more than sufficient, just to bear him through the fearful strife that awaited him, without his being broken or destroyed – so that he might experience, in all the faculties of his soul and body, the innumerable sensations of overpowering difficulty, and exhausting toil, and fainting weakness, and tormenting anguish, though by the Holy Ghost preserved from sin – and might touch the very brink of danger, though not be swept away by it, and feel all the horrors of the precipice, but without falling over.'[120] In fact M'Lagan stresses that Christ faced temptation with exactly the same resources as ourselves. He takes up the common objection, 'O! But in him was Godhead – and he had the promise of the Father that he should not fail nor be discouraged until his mighty task was completed!' The objection is quickly dismissed: 'And is not Godhead also your refuge and your strength, a very present help in the time of trouble? Does not the Holy Spirit dwell also in you? and has not the Father said to you also, "Fear not, for I am with thee: Be not dismayed, for I am thy God; I will strengthen thee, yea, I will help thee, yea, I will uphold thee with the right hand of my righteousness?" '

M'Lagan also advanced the initially startling idea that Jesus experienced a sense of weakness far beyond anything we can ever imagine. He illustrated this from the field of human conflict. On the threshold of battle, the monarch feels a far greater sense of insufficiency than the common soldier precisely because he exercises far greater powers and bears greater responsibilities. 'Even so,' he writes, 'we may understand how Christ, in possessing the most glorious powers, can yet have had a sense of weakness more deep and affecting by far than we, in the narrowness of our faculties, can either experience or conceive; a sense entirely suited to the unparalleled greatness and terror of his conflict. *He* saw the conjuncture in all its awful magnitude! He viewed the result in all its tremendous importance! He knew himself advancing to a post where his created and mortal nature, struck with the fiery darts of hell from beneath, and pierced from above by the arrows of the Almighty, must abide the shock and pressure of a falling world; and where the failure but for one moment of his *human* endurance and resolution, must effect not only the universal and eternal triumph of wickedness and misery; but what it is fearful to name, even while we know it can never happen – the defeat of his Father's counsel – the failure of his Father's truth – and the desecration of his Father's Godhead!'[121]

Other aspects of the incarnation were probed equally perceptively by the older Scottish theologians. A few examples must suffice.

First, Samuel Rutherford on the unipersonality of Christ: 'Christ's manhood has a personality, not of its own, but of the Godhead.'[122]

Secondly, John Maclaurin on the cry of dereliction: 'There was never a request for pity till now; he sought none from Pilate, he would have none from the sympathising daughters of Jerusalem...; but now he who was like a sheep dumb before the shearers, is dumb no more, and the Lamb being brought to this dreadful slaughter, must open his mouth, and Pity itself cries for pity. It was the upbraiding language of his murderers, What was become of his God? No wonder the world grew dark, and the rocks rent, to hear the blessed Jesus forced in appearance to join with them, to hear anything like the language of his murderers coming from his own mouth, That his God had forsaken him. When we consider how much a son will suffer from a father, or even from a friend whom he loves, before he divulge it to others, especially before enemies, it may make us reflect how much Christ suffered from God, when he who loved him so much, expressed his sufferings from him in such a manner before such company.'[123]

Thirdly, William Cunningham on the role of the Virgin Mother: 'she contributed to the formation of Christ's human nature just what mothers ordinarily contribute to the formation of their children.'[124] Cunningham probably borrowed this form of words from Marcus Dods who, a few years earlier, had used almost the same terms: 'the contagion of the fall excepted, she imparted to her Son all that other mothers import to their children.'[125]

Fourth, John Duncan on the limitations of our Lord's know-ledge: 'Ignorance is a defect, nescience is not a necessary defect. Christ was nescient, but not ignorant; for the latter is that beyond which there is a better – not only absolutely but relatively; better that is, for a particular state. Now there is a better state than nescience absolutely; but not relatively to man.'[126]

Finally, Hugh Martin's treatment of *kenosis* in a superb series of sermons on the Passion, 'This was the precise nature of his abasement,' wrote Martin, 'that though it was no robbery for him to be equal with God, he yet laid aside the reputation though never the reality thereof; and, remaining still, as he must ever remain, the same God unchangeable, he yet appeared in the form of a servant, not drawing on his divine might and energies, but denying himself their exercises and forth-putting – concealing, retiring out of view, withdrawing from the field of action, those prerogatives and powers of Deity, which in the twinkling of an eye might have scattered ten thousand worlds and hells of enemies. He withdrew them all from action that he might taste the weakness of created nature. And in thus denying himself the consolation and energy and support which the action of his divine upon his human nature, had he chosen, would have furnished to him boundlessly, in *this* consisted the test and trial of his submission to his Father's yoke, in the body which he had prepared him. To draw unduly on the resources of his Godhead, and in a manner inconsistent with his relation and his duty towards the Father, as the Mediator between God and man in the days of his flesh, was precisely that act to which the devil in vain sought to tempt him... for Jesus to have done so would have been to "make himself" of *some* "reputation".'[127]

What Martin was setting forth was not the idea of a mere *krupsis* (veiling) of Christ's divine powers but a real *kenosis*, involving a real self-denial and a real self-limitation. Christ assumed a nature and a position in which nothing but faith could have sustained him.[128] Indeed, he entered so fully into our humanness that in Gethsemane he longed earnestly to escape from his sufferings;[129] so fully that prayer was as truly indispensable to him as to any of his people: 'For in his resignation of all right to wield at pleasure the powers of his own Godhead, he "became poor" as his own poor and needy children, and left for himself only what *they* may ever draw upon – the fulness of the Father's Godhead and his promises.'[130]

But perhaps no one epitomised the historic Christology of Scotland better than William Guthrie of Fenwick, in his description of faith: 'now the heart is so enlarged for Him, as that less cannot satisfy, and more is not desired.... The soul now resolves to die if He shall so command, yet at His door, and looking towards Him.'[131]

References

1. *Writings of Edward Irving* (London: Alexander Strahan, 1865), Vol. V, pp. 3-446.

2. *Ibid*, p. 126.

3. *Ibid*., p. 129. *Memoirs of the Life, Times and Writings of Thomas Boston* (New edition, Glasgow, 1899), p. 402..

4. Adam Gib, *The Present Truth: A Display of the Secession Testimony* (Edinburgh: Fleming and Neill, 1774), Vol. I, p. 44.

5. *Ibid*., p. 99.

6. *The Collected*

7. *Ibid*., p. 137.

8. *Ibid*., p. 121.

9. *Ibid*., p. 141.

10. G. Strachan, *The Pentecostal Theology of Edward Irving* (London: Darton, Longman and Todd, 1973), p. 27.

11. *Ibid*., p. 28.

12. Irving, *Collected Writings*, Vol. V, p. 115.

13. *Ibid*., p. 116.

14. *Ibid*., p. 128.

15. *Ibid*., p. 136.

16. *Ibid*., p. 170.

17. *Ibid*., p. 563.

18. *Ibid*., p. 563.

19. *Ibid*., p. 564.

20. *Ibid*., p. 564.

21. Marcus Dods, *The Incarnation of the Eternal Word* (London: Seeley, Burnside & Seeley, Second Edition, 1845), p. ix.

22. A.B. Bruce, *The Humiliation of Christ* (Edinburgh: T & T Clark, 1876), pp. 269 ff.

23. K. Barth, *Church Dogmatics* (Edinburgh: T & T Clark, 1956), Vol. I.2, p. 153.

24. *Ibid*., p. 152.

25. Eberhard Busch, *Karl Barth: His Life from Letters and Autobiographical Texts* (London: SCM Press, 1976), p. 205.

26. H.R. Mackintosh, *The Person of Jesus Christ* (Edinburgh: T & T Clark, Second Edition, 1913), pp. 466 f.

27. *Ibid*, p. 473.

28. *Ibid*, pp. 473 f.

29. *Ibid*, pp. 476 f.

30. *Ibid*., p. 477.

31. *Ibid*., p. 477.

32. *Ibid*., p. 477.

33. *Ibid*., p. 478.

34. *Ibid*., p. 478.

35. *Ibid*., p. 479.

36. *Ibid*., p. 481.

37. *Ibid*., p. 481.

38. R.R. Redman Jr., 'H.R. Mackintosh's Contribution to Christology,' (*Scottish Journal of Theology*, Vol. 41, No. 4, 1988), pp. 517-534.

39. Donald Baillie, *God Was in Christ* (London: Faber and Faber, 1948), p. 11.

40. *Ibid*., p. 58.

42. W. Temple, *Christus Veritas* (London: Macmillan, 1925), pp. 142 f.

42. *Ibid.*, p. 97.

43. *Ibid.*, p. 87.

44. H.M. Relton, *A Study in Christology* (London: S.P.C.K., 1922).

45. Donald Baillie, *God Was in Christ*, p. 151.

46. *Ibid.*, p. 117.

47. I have in fact explored it a little more fully in *The Person of Christ* (Leicester: Inter-Varsity Press, 1998), pp. 190-92.

48. *Ibid.*, p. 149.

49. J.G. Machen, *Christianity and Liberalism* (London: Victory Press, 1923), pp. 83f.

50. E. Hoskyns and F.N. Davey, *The Riddle of the New Testament* (London: Faber and Faber, 1958).

51. A. Harnack, *What is Christianity?* (London: Williams and Norgate, 1904), p.147.

52. *Ibid.*, p. 148.

53. *Ibid.*, p. 150.

54. James Denney, *Jesus and the Gospel* (London: Hodder and Stoughton, 1908), p.12.

55. Denney, *Op. cit*, p. 104.

56. Denney, *Op.cit.,* p. 374.

57. P.W. Schniedel, *Encyclopaedia Biblica*, 1899-1903, Vol II, columns 1872 ff.

58. Denney, *op.cit.*, p. 171.

59. Denney, *op. cit.,* p. 188.

60. See A. McGrath, *The Making of Modern German Christology* (Oxford: Oxford University Press, 1986), pp. 16 ff.

61. Denney, *op. cit.*, p. 375.

62. *Ibid.*, p. 376.

63. *Ibid.*, p. 377.

64. *Ibid.*, p. 377.

65. *Ibid.*, p. 378.

66. *Ibid.*, p. 380.

67. *Ibid.*, p. 384.

68. *Ibid.*, pp. 391 f.

69. *Ibid.*, p. 403.

70. T.H. Darlow, *William Robertson Nicoll: Life and Letters*, p. 360.

71. *Ibid.*, p. 361.

72. *Ibid.*, p. 362.

73. *Ibid.*, p. 363.

74. *Ibid.*, p. 364.

75. J. Denney, *The Epistles to the Thessalonians* (London: Hodder and Stoughton, 1892), p.

76. R. Bultmann, *The Theology of the New Testament*, Vol. I, p. 129.

77. J. Denney in *The Expositor's Greek Testament*, ed. W. Robertson Nicoll (London: Hodder and Stoughton, 1904), Vol. II, p. 659.

78. *Ibid.*, p. 658.

79. J. Denney, *Studies in Theology* (London: Hodder and Stoughton, 1894), pp. 47-73.

80. B.F. Westcott, *The Gospel according to St. John* (London: , 1896) p. 3.

81. *William Robertson Nicoll: Life and Letters*, p. 364.

82. T.F. Torrance (Ed.), *The Incarnation* (Edinburgh: Handsel Press, 1991), p. xii.

83. *Ibid.*, p. xv.

84. T.F. Torrance, *The Mediation of Christ* (Grand Rapids: Eerdmans, 1984), p. 64.

85. T.F. Torrance (Ed.), *The Incarnation*, p. xx.

86. T.F. Torrance, *The School of Faith* (London: James Clarke, 1959), p. lxxiii.

87. T.F. Torrance, *Theology in Reconciliation* (London: Geoffrey Chapman, 1975), pp. 139-214.

88. *Ibid.*, p. 152.

89. *Ibid.*, p. 174.

90. T.F. Torrance, *The Mediation of Christ*, pp. 48 f.

91. *Ibid.*, p. 53.

92. *Ibid.*, pp. 48 f.

93. T.F. Torrance, *Theology in Reconciliation*, p. 153.

94. A. Harnack, *History of Dogma* (New York: Dover Publications, 1961), p. 45.

95. R.P.C. Hanson, *The Search for the Christian Doctrine of God* (Edinburgh: T&T Clark, 1988), p.451.

96. G.L. Prestige, *Fathers and Heretics* (London: S.P.C.K., 1940), p. 115.

97. J. Calvin, *Commentary on the Epistle to the Romans* (Edinburgh: Calvin Translation Society, 1844), p. 198.

98. K. Barth, *The Epistle to the Romans* (London: Oxford University Press, 1933), p. 279.

99. J. Knox, *The Humanity and Divinity of Jesus Christ* (Cambridge: Cambridge University Press, 1967), p. 33.

100. Edward Irving, *Collected Writings*, Vol. V, p. 565.

101. T. F. Torrance, *The School of Faith*, p. lxxxvi.

102. T.F. Torrance, *Theology in Reconstruction* (London: SCM Press, 1965), p. 155.

103. T.F. Torrance, *The Mediation of Christ*, p. 79.

104. Robert Bruce, *The Mystery of the Lord's Supper*, ed. T.F. Torrance (London: James Clarke, 1958), p. 35.

105. T.F. Torrance, *Theology in Reconciliation*, p. 153.

106. Edward Irving, *Collected Writings*, Vol. V, p. 115.

107. *Ibid.*, pp. 563 f.

108. *Ibid.*, pp. 123 f.

109. *Ibid.*, p. 566.

110. T.F. Torrance, *Theology in Reconstruction*, p. 157.

111. *Ibid.*, p. 158.

112. *Ibid.*, p. 159.

113. T.F. Torrance, *Theology in Reconciliation*, p. 139.

114. Alexander Stewart, *The Tree of Promise* (Edinburgh: William P. Kennedy, 1864), pp. 31 f.

115. *Ibid.*, p. 78.

116. *Ibid.*, p. 81.

117. James M'Lagan, *A Sermon on Hebrews* IV.15 appended to Marcus Dods' *On the Incarnation of the Word*, pp. 289-306.

118. *Ibid.*, p. 290.

119. *Ibid.*, p. 397.

120. *Ibid.*, p. 300.

121. *Ibid.*, p. 302.

122. Samuel Rutherford, *Fourteen Communion Sermons*, ed. A.A. Bonar (Glasgow: Charles Glass & Co., Second Edition, 1877, p. 111.

123. John Maclaurin, from 'God's Chief Mercy', a sermon published in *The Works of the late John Maclaurin* (Edinburgh: Waugh and Innes, 1818), Vol. I, p. 132.

124. W. Cunningham, *Historical Theology* (Edinburgh: T. & T. Clark, 1862), Vol. I, p. 313.

125. Marcus Dods, *On the Incarnation of the Word*, p. 31.

126. J. Duncan, *Colloquia Peripatetica* (Edinburgh: Edmoston & Douglas, Third Edition, 1871), pp. 26 f.

127. H. Martin, *the Shadow of Calvary* (Glasgow: Free Presbyterian Publications, 1954), p. 26.

128. *Ibid.*, p. 63.

129. *Ibid.*, p. 22.

130. *Ibid.*, p. 55.

131. William Guthrie, *The Christian's Great Interest* (Glasgow: Free Presbyterian Publications, 1951) p. 43

6

THE CHRISTOLOGY OF JURGEN MOLTMANN*

Of Dr. Jurgen Moltmann's many publications only one, *The Way of Jesus Christ*, is specifically devoted to Christology.[1] All the others, however, have significant Christological content. This is certainly true of the two other volumes of what he himself labelled his 'systematic contributions to theology':[2] *The Trinity and the Kingdom of God* (1980) and *God in Creation* (1985). But it is equally true of his earlier works: *Theology of Hope* (1964), *The Crucified God* (1972) and *The Church in the Power of the Spirit* (1975).[3]

Between the earlier and later works there are, however, clear shifts in emphasis. Moltmann himself admits that by 1980 he no longer wanted to be controversial and decided to focus instead on 'long-term problems of theology'.[4] But the changes appear to be merely changes of emphasis. There have been no retractions.

Moltmann is not an easy read. One reason for this is that all his works are involved simultaneously in several different discourses. Feminism, ecology, anti-semitism, theodicy, the peace movement and political activism are never far out of sight even when he is discussing Christology. These peripheral conversations are always fascinating, but they are also distracting, especially since the reader faces the further difficulty that Moltmann's work does not run in the tram-lines of conventional theological debate. His Christology, for example, does not follow the contours of biblical theology, plotting the New Testament development. Nor does it engage seriously with historical theology. In *The Way of Jesus Christ* Moltmann achieves the extraordinary feat of writing over 300 pages on Christology without once mentioning Chalcedon. Nor, again, does he follow the categories of systematic theology. The student who looks for the classic *loci* (pre-existence, incarnation, unipersonality and so on) may indeed find something, but she

---

* This chapter first appeared in *Themelios*, Vol. 24, No. 2 (February 1999).

will have to search carefully, and as she searches she will be
conscious of few landmarks.

This is linked to a further difficulty: verification. How does
Moltmann satisfy himself that something is true? More important,
how does he convince the reader that something is true? The two
means of verification normally open to Christians are Scripture
and tradition. Neither of these seems particularly important to
Moltmann. He has a decidedly smorgasbord approach to the canon;
and his respect for fathers and reformers is scant, to say the least.
His real criteria lie elsewhere. In order to be true, a doctrine must
offer a viable theodicy (it must shed light on Auschwitz); it must
advance Jewish-Christian dialogue, bearing in mind that Jews were
'sufferers' and Christians 'perpetrators'; it must meet the
ecological concerns of mankind; it must give a platform for
Christian political activism; and it must both illuminate and be
illuminated by the preoccupations of feminism. Above all,
theological statements must be validated by experience.[5] Even
what looks like his fundamental theological principle, *crux probat
omnia* ('the cross is the test of everything') is itself accepted only
because it conforms to these criteria.

But the main reason for the reader's difficulty is that Moltmann
never allows us to relax. It is as if he were determined that every
sentence had to be either provocative, brilliant or questionable.
Reviewers have spoken variously of 'subtle complexity', 'minute
complexity' and 'comprehensive profusion'. The argument often
proceeds by way of image and suggestion rather than by way of
clarification and analysis. As a result, the reader is liable to go
away stimulated, yet less enlightened than he thinks.

Yet there are some ideas hammered out so relentlessly and set
in so many different lights that they become for ever part of our
theological baggage. Two of these are particularly important: first,
Jesus as the fulfilment of the Messianic hope; secondly, Jesus as
the crucified God.

Jesus and the messianic hope

Moltmann's stress on eschatology was stated unmistakeably in
his first major publication, *Theology of Hope*. Christianity, he

argued, is not only *evangelion* but *epangelia*: not only 'good news' but 'promise'. Furthermore, *evangelion* itself has to be taken not primarily as good news about the past but as good news about the future. This is closely connected with Christ's resurrection, which Moltmann discusses in the core section of *Theology of Hope* (Chapter III, 'The Resurrection and the Future of Jesus Christ'). Modern reflection on this topic, he notes, has been preoccupied with the question, Is it historical? For post-enlightenment man the answer has been, No! Even Christians have tended to see the story of the resurrection not as a statement about an event, but as a statement about their own state of mind. Behind this lies the principle espoused by such scholars as Troeltsch: history is analogical. All historical events are basically similar and the threshold criterion by which we are to judge whether an event is historical is its agreement 'with normal, usual, or at least variously attested happenings'.[6]

If we approach the gospel accounts of the resurrection armed with this criterion we shall, of course, conclude that they are un-historical. But there is an alternative way, argues Moltmann. The resurrection itself challenges and questions our whole modern understanding of what is 'historical'. In particular, it challenges Troeltsch's principle of analogy and sheds revolutionary new light on what is historically possible. Hence its central importance. The debate about it is no mere wrangle over a detail of the distant past. It is concerned with the nature of history itself. Christ did not simply repeat the past. Neither will Christian history merely repeat the past. The parousia will bring something new: something that has never happened before, even in Christ. The resurrection tells us that history is governed not by analogy, but by (divine) promise.

Moltmann's forthright emphasis on the resurrection[7] presents a curious contrast to his attitude to the virgin birth, which he dismisses as a legend (or set of legends) created to give mythical expression to the idea of Jesus as the divine Son. It is difficult to see why a view of history shaped by the resurrection cannot equally accommodate the virgin birth. Once we breach the principle that all historical events are analogous we surely have an epistemological framework for all the Christian miracles. If so, then the miracle of Christmas performs the same function at the beginning of Jesus' life as the wonder of the empty tomb does at its end.[8]

The all-embracing emphasis on eschatology in *Theology of Hope* is sharply focused on Christology in *The Way of Jesus Christ*. Moltmann admits (page xiii) that he wrestled over the choice of title. 'Way,' he says, is evocative of three ideas: process (or progress) as applied to Jesus himself; development, as the church's own Christological advances in a historically conditioned and limited environment; and ethics, as the gospel invites us to follow the way of Jesus.

It is the first of these ideas that dominates Moltmann's Christology. He is concerned with the eschatological journey of Jesus. It is not, however, a solitary journey. It is a trinitarian one: the story is the story of Jesus' dealings with the Father and Jesus' dealings with the Spirit as, together, they redeem and renew creation.

Jesus' *Way*, according to Moltmann, is in three stages: the messianic fulfilment in the Advent; the apocalyptic sufferings of Messiah at Calvary; and the messianic consummation in the final renewal of the cosmos.

The first of these, the messianic advent, is obviously pivotal. For Moltmann, the central Christological concept is *messiahship*. He lays down the challenge, 'What does christology mean except messianology?' (page 1) and goes on to build on the fact that the Gospels understand his whole coming and ministry in the contexts of Israel's messianic hope (page 28). First and foremost, then, Jesus is the one in whom Old Testament and Jewish expectations find their fulfilment (Moltmann does not seriously consider the possibility that Old Testament promise and Jewish expectation may have diverged radically). Hence his choice of sub-title: *Christology in Messianic Dimensions.*

From such a standpoint Moltmann is inevitably dismissive of the *anthropological* Christology which in German Liberalism ended up merely admiring 'Rabbi Jesus' and in British Modernism tended towards equating the human with the divine (Christ was truly God because he was truly man). He is more ambivalent towards patristic Christology. One of his central concerns, after all, is with what the Way of Jesus means for God and this inevitably requires an acceptance of trinitarianism. At the same time, he is sharply critical of both the Apostles' and Nicene Creed on the ground that they present a static Christology focused on metaphysical concepts such as *nature* and *substance*. As a result, they have virtually nothing to say on 'the Way' of Jesus. They are silent on his earthly life and ministry and on his prophetic and social teaching. Even the Apostles' Creed moves directly from 'was born' to 'suffered under Pontius Pilate', as if there was nothing in between.[9]

Moltmann is deeply conscious that *messiahship* is a Jewish concept and that any claim that Jesus is the Messiah must refer in the first instance to his being the Jewish Messiah (there is no other) and the fulfilment of Jewish hope. This raises a question of critical importance: Why does the Jew say 'No!' to Jesus? Moltmann cites a number of Jewish scholars (most notably Martin Buber) to provide an answer. They say, 'Jesus has not fulfilled our hope! The world is not redeemed! And we do not see the life and work of Jesus as constituting any real caesura in human history!'[10]

At the heart of these objections lies a radically different view of redemption. According to Buber, 'The redemption of the world is for us indivisibly one with the perfecting of creation.'[11] Schalom Ben-Chorin speaks to the same effect: 'The Jew is profoundly aware of the unredeemed character of the world.'[12]

Part of Moltmann's answer is that Judaism has its own embarrassments. Ben-Chorin, for example, argues that the only caesura in history is the giving of the Torah on Mount Sinai. But this, too, says Moltmann, left the world unredeemed. Similarly, if there can be no provisional messianic presence in an unredeemed world, what room is there for the quasi-messianic presence of 'the chosen people'?

But Moltmann's real answer is to accept the premises of the Jewish argument and then proceed to assimilate it into his Christology. Jesus has not fulfilled the hope of Israel: yet.

The 'yet' is crucial. Jesus has still to complete his way and finish his journey. Moltmann even suggests that he is not yet Messiah. It is something he is becoming or working his way into.

Such language surely confuses the holding of an office with the completion of its task: Tony Blair *is*, presumably, Prime Minister? But Moltmann's central contention is both true and invaluable. The fact that Christ has not completed his task does not discredit him. He is on the way to completing it and in his *parousia* he will give us all that the Jew ever longed for. In particular, he will give us that new creation which is central to Jewish hope. The kingdom of God will ultimately mean the transformation of the whole of reality. We have no right to interiorise it (as if it had significance only for personal religion) or to politicise it (as in the state-allied churches of Christendom). It is external, material and social, involving both a universal reign of peace and a perfected creation. Moltmann's favourite text is 1 Corinthians 15:28: God will be all in all. Unfortunately, he never exegetes it and one hesitates to do the exegesis for him. The best provisional exegesis is the Lord's Prayer: when the Messiah finishes his journey, God's will will be done on earth as it is in heaven.

This central emphasis on messianic Christology is profoundly satisfying. At its edges, however, there are several questions.

One was raised by Karl Barth shortly after the publication of *Theology of Hope* in 1964. 'This new systematising,' wrote Barth, 'is almost too good to be true.'[13] If anything, this is even more true of *The Way of Jesus Christ,* and the situation is further complicated by the fact that in Moltmann's thought there are also parallel systems (and systems within systems). For example, behind the dominant arrangement in *The Way of Jesus Christ* we find a further schematisation under the heading, 'The Three-Dimensional Person of Jesus Christ' (page 149). The three dimensions are (1) his eschatological person (2) his theological person and (3) his social person. It is difficult to assess such patterns. Does their multiplicity serve to prevent the hegemony of any single one? Or does their abundance reflect a mind disposed to impose order and classification where none exist?

Barth also expressed the opinion that Moltmann's hope is 'finally only a principle and thus a vessel with no contents'.[14] This observation was linked to the influence on Moltmann of Ernst Bloch, a Marxist exponent of the philosophy of hope ('hope without God'). Moltmann read Bloch's work, *The Principle of Hope*, in 1960 while on holiday in Switzerland and later confessed, 'I was so fascinated that I ceased to see the beauty of the mountains.'[15] Barth suspected that Moltmann simply wanted to 'baptise' Bloch, but Moltmann vigorously denied this: 'I did not seek to be Bloch's heir.'[16]

Moltmann could offer a strong case in his own defence, especially since he links the fulfilment of hope very closely to the parousia. Against Barth's tendency to speak of the parousia as merely a revelation of what Christ already is, Moltmann insists that it brings in something new. 'Christ's parousia,' he writes, 'does not merely "unveil" the salvific meaning of Christ's death. It also, and much more, brings the *fulfilment* of the whole history of Christ, with all that it promises; for it is only with Christ's parousia that "the kingdom that shall have no end" begins.... That is why this future of Christ does not bring the turn of history "once more"; it brings it "once and for all".'[17]

More serious is the objection that Moltmann's stress on eschatology is secured at the expense of the cross. Beneath this lies something more fundamental still: Moltmann's passion for theodicy betrays him into being obsessed with suffering almost to the exclusion of sin. It is God who has the problem, not man. Why did he permit Auschwitz or Hiroshima? The sense of guilt and the classic Lutheran preoccupation with forgiveness and justification are almost entirely absent. The quest is for answers, not for forgiveness; for hope, not for acquittal.[18] Even the cross is an affirmation of God's solidarity with us in pain, rather than a divine act of atonement for sin. In fact, Christ would have come even if man had never sinned. As a result, Moltmann is totally dismissive of the Anselmic view of the incarnation as what he calls 'an emergency measure ... the functional presupposition for the atoning sacrifice on the cross'.[19]

Moltmann finds the rationale of the incarnation not in sin, but in creation. At one level, it is the perfected self-communication of the triune God to his world.[20] At another, it is a step taken 'for the sake of perfecting creation'.[21] This is linked to some dubious exegesis of the reference in Genesis 1:26-27 to man's being made in the image of God. Moltmann takes this as a promise: in Christ 'we have the fulfilment of the promise made to man that he will be "the image of the invisible God".' It follows from this, according to Moltmann, that Christ is the true man and 'it is therefore in union with him that believers discover the truth of human existence'.[22] In other words, even if man had never fallen Christ would still have become incarnate in order that we should have a clear idea of what was meant by being in the image of God. Such reasoning has only a tenuous link with the biblical text and falls completely apart if the image was a fact of history rather than a part of eschatology (that is, if man at his point of origin was made in the image of God). Besides, such a demonstration of the image would have been absolutely useless for all the generations before the incarnation. They would have had no inkling of what was meant by the image of God.

As an appendix to this we should note Moltmann's assumption that on the Anselmic view Christ becomes redundant after the cross: once creation has been redeemed the God-man is no longer needed.[23] But this is not a natural consequence of the Anselmic view. The soteriological work of Christ continues between the resurrection and the parousia; and even after the parousia Christ continues as the Last Adam, the head of creation and the first-born among many brethren. He will function for ever as the pastor of his people (Rev. 7:17); and he is the designated leader of humanity in its stewardship of the ages (Heb. 2:9).

The Crucified God

The second outstanding idea in Moltmann's Christology is the divine suffering involved in the life of Christ and particularly in his cross. This is usually associated with what will probably remain his *magnum opus*, *The Crucified God*, but it also figures prominently in *The Trinity and the Kingdom of God* (Chapter II, 'The Passion of God') and in *The Way of Jesus Christ* (Chapter IV, 'The Apocalyptic Sufferings of Christ').

The Crucified God was published in 1972. 'I wrote it,' said Moltmann later, 'with my lifeblood.'[24] More than any other of his works it reflects his personal vision of the theological task: 'For me theology springs from a divine passion – it is the open wound of God in one's own life and in the tormented men, women and children of this world.'[25] Like the earlier work, *Theology of Hope*, it sees the whole of theology from a focal point: 'For me the cross of Christ became the "foundation and critique of Christian theology".'[26] In particular, Moltmann wished to change from what he saw as the traditional preoccupation with what the cross meant for Jesus to what he saw as a revolutionary preoccupation with what it means for God: 'Does an impassible God keep silent in heaven untouched by the suffering and death of his child on Golgotha, or does God himself suffer these pains and this death?'[27] At the same time, Moltmann remained committed to his quest for a theodicy. '*The Crucified God*,' he wrote, 'was also my attempt to find an answer for a life in Germany after Auschwitz.'[28]

At the heart of *The Crucified God* lies an emphatic rejection of the idea of divine impassibility (here Moltmann acknowledges his debt to British thinkers such as J.K. Mozley, G.A. Studdart Kennedy and C.E. Rolt, as well as to Kazoh Kitamori, Miguel de Unamuno and, of course, Dietrich Bonhoeffer, who once wrote in his prison cell, 'Only the suffering God can help'). Moltmann defines his position carefully. God cannot suffer unwillingly or helplessly. Neither can he suffer because of any deficiency in his being. Nor, again, can he ever be mere victim, helplessly assailed. But he can suffer *actively*, argues Moltmann. He can go towards suffering and accept it. He can suffer in love. This does not bespeak any deficiency in his being. On the contrary, it is possible only because of 'the fulness of his being, i.e. his love'.[29] He is affected by human actions and sufferings not because he is afflicted by some neurosis but because 'he is interested in his creation, his people and his right'.[30]

To some extent Moltmann can appeal (and does appeal) to the prophets in support of his denial of impassibility. He writes, for example, 'At the heart of the prophetic proclamation there stands the certainty that God is interested in the world to the point of suffering.'[31] But his real appeal is to the cross. He invokes Luther's principle, *crux probat omnia* ('the cross is the test of everything') and argues that the simplistic idea that God cannot suffer is

exploded at Calvary. The cross is not merely something which
happens to Christ. It happens between him and his Father.
Moltmann is careful to reject Patripassianism. It is not the Father
who was crucified, dead and buried. The suffering of the Father,
he insists, was different from that of the Son. But it was no less
real. What Abraham did not do to Isaac, God did to his own Son.
He gave him up. He abandoned him. He cast him out. He delivered
him to an accursed death. In doing so, the Father himself 'suffers
the death of the Son in the infinite grief of love'.[32] Having said
that, Moltmann instantly warns against understanding the Father's
suffering in theopaschitic terms. The cross is not the death of God.
God did not die. He did not cease to exist or cease to function. We
must speak not of the death *of* God but of death *in* God.[33] More
precisely, we must speak in trinitarian terms: 'The Son suffers
dying, the Father suffers the death of the Son.... The Fatherlessness
of the Son is matched by the Sonlessness of the Father.'[34] What
they share is that each *surrenders*. The Son surrenders himself to
forsakenness. The Father surrenders his Son. Most deeply separated
in the forsakenness, they are most inwardly one in surrendering.

Here then, just where he seems most decisively eclipsed, God
is most clearly revealed. Precisely where the Father and the Son
are separated we see the divine story as one which is essentially
trinitarian: 'if the cross of Christ is understood as a divine event,
i.e. as an event between Jesus and his God and Father, it is
necessary to speak in trinitarian terms of the Son and the Father
and the Spirit.... The form of the crucified Christ is the Trinity.'[35]
No doubt Moltmann is striving, as usual, to make his language as
striking and innovative as possible. But, clarified and analysed, it
seems fully consonant with what B. B. Warfield wrote eighty years
ago: the revelation of the trinity 'was made not in word but in
deed. It was made in the incarnation of God the Son, and the
outpouring of God the Holy Spirit ... the revelation of the Trinity
was incidental to, and the inevitable effect of, the accomplishment
of redemption.'[36]

But the cross revolutionises ('modifies', to use Warfield's word)
our concept of God not only to the extent of defining him as triune
but also to the extent of shattering the idea of divine impassibility.

Many Christians have difficulty with this, but it seems to me that Moltmann's central concern (what the cross meant for God the Father) accords fully with the perspectives of the New Testament itself. There, the key-texts (John 3:16, Romans 5:8, Romans 8:32, 1 John 4:9f.) see Calvary not merely, or even primarily, as an action of God the Son but as an action of God the Father. It is first and foremost a demonstration of *his* love. However important the priesthood of the Son, the priesthood of the Father is primary. It is the cost to *him*, as the one who gave up his Son, that is stressed.

Moltmann espouses the dialectical (as opposed to the analogical) principle in his approach to the knowledge of God. Being is revealed not in its like but in its opposite. Love, for example, is revealed only in hatred, and unity only in conflict. Similarly God is revealed only in his opposite. The god-ness of God appears only in the paradox of divine abandonment on Calvary. There is truth in this to the extent that the concept of God which emerges from Calvary is counter-intuitive. Our personal *sensus deitatis* does not expect divine kenosis or divine passibility. That is why such an idea is a *scandalon*. But this is no reason to reject the principle of analogy. Indeed, it is analogy which offers the best framework for the defence of passibility. *We* could not sacrifice our own children without pain. Abraham could not sacrifice Isaac without pain. If we are made in God's image (which we undoubtedly are, although Moltmann views this as only a hope), we can extrapolate from what Calvary would have cost ourselves to what it cost God: all the more so because the New Testament language of the cross deliberately echoes Abraham's experience. In the accounts of both the Baptism and the Transfiguration Jesus, like Isaac, is 'my Son, whom I love' (Matt. 3:17; 17:5). If the sacrifice cost God nothing, if he surrendered his Son impassively and unmovedly, he is utterly different from us and we are not in his image. If there was for him no pain and no cost, if Calvary was a mere blip on the impersonal screen of the Unmoved Mover, we are not in his image. It is not merely that we cannot attain to such Stoicism: we deplore and abhor it. It would mean that he is not love and that Fatherhood and Sonship are optional, meaningless metaphors.[37]

What Moltmann does not do justice to, however, is the anomalousness of the divine pain. 'The self-sacrifice of love,' he writes, 'is God's eternal nature'.[38] This gives the divine pain a degree of inevitability and normality which does not do justice to the perspectives of grace or to the discretionary nature of mercy. Nor does it take proper account of the reasons behind our instinctive aversion to the idea of divine passibility. Our instinct is that it is inconceivable that 'the blessed God' should suffer stress, disturbance or commotion. It is unthinkable that a frown should cross his face or a furrow wrinkle his brow. We know that in a normal universe God would be impassible. But the universe is not normal. It has been disrupted by sin; and sin is *anomia* (1 John 3:4). Once that *anomia* enters history it carries a thousand other anomalies in its train. It involves the whole creation in suffering. It involves God in the alien, distasteful work of condemnation. And it involves God in pain.

Any theodicy which relieves this tension is *ipso facto* discredited. Sin is that which absolutely ought not to be; and pain in God is that which absolutely ought not to be. The Crucified God is unthinkable. Sin (*anomia*) makes it possible, but nothing makes it logical, far less self-evident. Moltmann is open to Anselm's charge, *Nondum considerasti quanti ponderis sit peccatum*.

Out of God's passion there arises, as Moltmann stresses, the divine sympathy. Through the incarnation God shares and understands our finitude. Through the cross, God enters our godforsakenness: 'He humbles himself and takes upon himself the eternal death of the godless and the godforsaken, so that all the godless and the godforsaken can experience communion with him.'[39] Hence 'the godforsaken and rejected man can accept himself when he comes to know the crucified God who is with him and has already accepted him.'[40] (One is slightly uneasy about the idea that this applies to *every* godforsaken man; but this is probably taken care of by the reference to his *coming to know* the crucified God. Nevertheless, Moltmann's thought shows a strong tendency towards universalism.)

This point about the divine sympathy is dramatically illustrated in a passage which Moltmann quotes from *Night*, a book written by E. Wiesel, a survivor of Auschwitz:

> The SS hanged two Jewish men and a youth in front of the whole camp. The men died quickly, but the death throes of the youth lasted for half an hour. 'Where is God? Where is he?' someone asked behind me. As the youth still hung in torment in the noose after a long time, I heard the man call again, 'Where is God now?' And I heard a voice in myself answer: 'Where is he? He is here. He is hanging there on the gallows ...'[41]

This is the idea of God's sympathy with the oppressed carried to its ultimate (and, I think, quite legitimate) conclusion. 'There cannot be any other Christian answer to the question of this torment,' writes Moltmann. 'To speak here of a God who could not suffer would make God a demon. To speak here of an absolute God would make God an annihilating nothingness.'[42]

Finally, Moltmann brings out with great clarity the fact that it was because of his prophetic ministry that Christ was crucified. The Gospels are not interested in his sufferings from nature and fate, or in his economic sufferings as a carpenter's son. They focus on those sufferings which he prompted by his actions. He 'incited' the world against himself 'by his message and the life that he lived'.[43]

This is the root of Moltmann's sympathy with Liberation Theology.[44] Christians, he insists, have no right to quote Jesus as an example of mere patience and submission to fate. Even less do we have a right to use him as an excuse for our own silence, passivity and weakness in the face of social injustice. 'Too often,' writes Moltmann, 'peasants, Indians and black slaves have been called upon by the representatives of the dominant religion to accept their sufferings as "their cross" and not to rebel against them.'[45] He pleads, instead (and in classic Liberation terminology), for an orthodoxy which is matched by *orthopraxis:* one which draws out the consequences of the cross for politics: 'The church of the crucified Christ must take sides in the concrete social and political conflicts going on about it and in which it is involved, and must be prepared to join and form parties.'[46]

That, however, is another question, for another time.

Finally, a caveat. As deconstructionists tirelessly remind us, every writer loses control over his work once it is published. To some extent, great or small, he is at the mercy of his reader, unable to dictate his response. Moltmann is more vulnerable than most. his work has been described as an invitation to think and to rethink. The danger is that we read with our own eyes, proceed to think and rethink our own thoughts and then attribute them to Moltmann. I doubt if I have escaped that hazard: in which case I must thank him for some of my own most cherished thoughts.

References

1. Moltmann offers a more popular treatment in *Jesus Christ for Today's World* (London: SCM Press, 1994).

2. Jurgen Moltmann, Ed., *How I Have Changed: Reflections on Thirty Years of Theology* (London: SCM Press, 1997), p.20.

3. Details of Moltmann's major publications are as follows: *Theology of Hope* (1965. ET, London, SCM Press, 1967); *The Crucified God* (1972. ET of 2nd edition, London, SCM Press, 1974); *The Church in the Power of the Spirit (1975.* ET, London, SCM Press, 1977); *The Trinity and the Kingdom of God (*1980. ET, London, SCM Press, 1981), *God in Creation* (1985. ET, London, SCM Press, 1985); *The Way of Jesus Christ* (1989. ET, London, SCM Press, 1990).

4. *How I Have Changed*, p.20.

5. In *Jesus Christ for Today's World*, for example, he observes (p.2) that 'practice is the touchstone against which a christology's authenticity has to be tested'. Cf. *How I Have Changed*, p.20: 'It should be possible to verify theological statements by one's own experiences or by empathy with the experiences of others.' But how, then are we to 'authenticate' practice and experience?

6. *Theology of Hope*, p.175.

7. He speaks more ambiguously in *Jesus Christ for Today's World* (p.4): 'Of course the symbols of raising and resurrection are drawn from an earlier era, when people talked in mythical pictures and images about God's marvellous intervention in this world.'

8. Cf., Karl Barth, *Church Dogmatics*, Vol. I, 2, pp.172- 184.

9. Moltmann suggests that the following might be inserted at this point in the Creed:
Baptised by John the Baptist
filled with the Holy Spirit
to proclaim God's kingdom to the poor
to heal the sick
to receive the rejected
to awaken Israel for the salvation of the nations
and to have mercy on all human beings.
(*Jesus Christ for Today's World*, pp.3-4).

10. *The Way of Jesus Christ*, pp.28-37.

11. Cited in *The Way of Jesus Christ*, p.28, from Martin Buber, *Der Jude und sein Judentum* (Cologne, 1963), p.562.

12. *The Way of Jesus Christ*, p. 29. Quoted from Schalom Ben-Chorin, *Die Antwort des Jona* (Hamburg, 1956), p.99.

13. Karl Barth, *Letters 1961-1968* (Edinburgh: T&T Clark, 1981), p.174.

14. Karl Barth, *Letters 1961-1968*, p.218.

15. Jurgen Moltmann, *How I Have Changed*, p.15.

16. Jurgen Moltmann, *How I Have Changed*, p.16.

17. Jurgen Moltmann, *The Way of Jesus Christ*, p.319.

18. Cf. the comment of Ruth Page (reviewing *The Trinity and the Kingdom of God*), 'Humanity seems to require perfecting in its fellowship rather than saving from its sin' (*Scottish Journal of Theology*, Vol. 37 No.1 [1984], p.98).

19. Jurgen Moltmann, *The Trinity and the Kingdom of God*, p.114.

20. *The Trinity and the Kingdom of God*, p.116.

21. *The Trinity and the Kingdom of God*, p.116.

22. *The Trinity and the Kingdom of God*, pp.116-7.

23. *The Trinity and the Kingdom of God*, p.115. Cf. the discussion of Calvin's idea of Christ as the *lieutenant de Dieu* in *The Crucified God*, pp. 257-262.

24. *How I Have Changed*, p.18.

25. J. Moltmann *et al.*, *A Passion for God's Reign* (Grand Rapids: Eerdmans, 1998), p.2

26. *How I Have Changed*, p.18.

27. *How I Have Changed*, p.18.

28. Cf. Hartmut Meesmann's remark that for Moltmann 'theology after Auschwitz must be different from theology before the annihilation of the Jews' (*How I Have Changed*, p.119).

29. *The Crucified God*, p.230.

30. *The Crucified God*, p.270.

31. *The Crucified God*, p.271.

32. *The Crucified God*, p.243.

33. It is probably true, however, that Moltmann flits too easily from the idea of God *suffering* to the idea of God *dying*. See D. G. Attfield's comments in 'Can God Be Crucified? A Discussion of J. Moltmann' (*Scottish Journal of Theology*, Vol. 30 No. 1 [1997], pp.49-50: 'there is no sense in attributing an absolute ending of body and brain process to the almighty ... God cannot therefore die in the sense of ceasing to be, and still be called God.'

34. *The Crucified God*, p.243.

35. *The Crucified God*, p.246.

36. B. B. Warfield, *Biblical and Theological Studies* (Philadelphia: Presbyterian and Reformed Publishing Company, 1952), p.33. The quotation is from an article, 'The Biblical Doctrine of the Trinity', first published in the *International Standard Bible Encyclopaedia* (Chicago, 1915), Vol. V, pp.3012-3022.

37. See *The Crucified God*, p.230: 'Were God incapable of suffering in any respect, and therefore in an absolute sense, then he would also be incapable of love.'

38. *The Trinity and the Kingdom of God*, p.32.

39. *The Crucified God*, p.276.

40. *The Crucified God*, p.277.

41. *The Crucified God*, pp.273-274. Quoted from E. Wiesel, *Night* (1969), pp.75f.

42. *The Crucified God*, p.274.

43. *The Crucified God*, p.51.

44. See *How I Have Changed*, p.19. Cf. *The Trinity and the Kingdom of God*, p.8: 'There must be no theology of liberation without the glorification of God and no glorification of God without the liberation of the oppressed.'

45. *The Crucified God*, p.49.

46. *The Crucified God*, p.53.

7

THE CHRISTOLOGY OF
WOLFHART PANNENBERG*

Wolfhart Pannenberg (born in 1928) began his career as a Professor of Theology at the University of Heidelberg. After brief spells first at Wuppertal (where he was colleague to Jurgen Moltmann) and then at Mainz he became Professor of Systematic Theology on the Protestant Faculty of the University of Munich in 1968. He retired in 1993.

Throughout his life, Pannenberg has had two major, inter-linked preoccupations. One has been the philosophy of history. The other has been Christology. The latter is the subject of his best-known monograph, *Jesus – God and Man*,[1] but it is also extensively covered in *The Apostles' Creed in the Light of Today's Questions*[2] and in Volume 2 of his *Systematic Theology*.[3]

Christology 'from below'

Pannenberg's name has come to be closely associated with the debate over the relative merits of a *Christology from above* and a *Christology from below*. The former was dominant in classical Christology from Ignatius to Chalcedon and finds modern representatives in Barth and Brunner.[4] It takes its starting-point in the eternal, pre-existent deity of Christ and sees it as the task of Christology (in the language of Barth) to describe the journey of the Son of God into the Far Country. Pannenberg, rather unfairly, compares Barth's position to the Gnostic Redeemer Myth (*Jesus*, 33), involving a circle of descent and ascent. But he also offers more solid criticisms:

First, a Christology from above presupposes the divinity of Jesus, whereas the primary task of Christology is to *vindicate* our confession of that divinity.

Secondly, a Christology that starts from above finds it hard to

---

* This chapter first appeared in *Themelios*, Vol. 25, No. 2 (February 2000).

do justice to the real, historical features of the man, Jesus of Nazareth. For example, it almost invariably shows little interest in his relationship with the Judaism of his day. Yet that relationship was definitive for his teaching and personality.

Thirdly, Christology from above, is, as far as we are concerned, a closed book: 'we would need to stand in the position of God himself in order to follow the way of God's Son into the world' (*Jesus,* 35).

By the same token, however, Pannenberg himself is precluded from a consistent 'Christology from below'. Such a Christology would have to assume that the study engaged in is concerned not only with a real man, but with a mere man, and would feel bound to account for everything in the life of Jesus without any recourse to the hypothesis of his divinity. Pannenberg cannot logically do that because before he is a theologian he is a believer. In effect, he is already looking at 'below' from above, approaching the whole task of Christology from the standpoint of the resurrection.

More important (and this is the strongest argument for a Christology from above), this is where the New Testament itself begins. Not only do the writers themselves set out from the standpoint of faith: their narratives characteristically start 'above'. This is most apparent in John's Prologue, the opening verses of the Epistle to the Hebrews and the Christ-Hymn in Philippians 2: 5-11. But it is also apparent in the Synoptic Gospels, including the earliest of them, the Gospel of Mark. His theme, as stated unashamedly in his opening sentence, is 'Jesus Christ, the Son of God'[5] and all the subsequent material merely expounds and illustrates this central thesis. This exactly parallels the approach of the Gospel of John: 'these things were written that you may believe that Jesus is the Christ, the Son of God' (John 20:31).

The same stand-point is reflected in Matthew and Luke. The former introduces Jesus as Immanuel; the latter as the Son of the Most High, the Son of David and the Son of God. Both writers clearly intend us to understand from the outset that it is no mere man who is the subject of the story that follows.

The virgin birth

In both Matthew and Luke, of course, the symbol of 'Christology from above' is the Virgin Birth. With this idea, Pannenberg has no patience, as can be seen from his treatment of the subject in *Jesus – God and Man*, 141-150.[6] He forthrightly denies its historicity, describes it as a legend and emphatically rejects Barth's attempt to place it on the same level as the resurrection. The two events, he argues, differ radically both in their historical basis and in their significance for Christianity. The story of the virgin birth originated in the Hellenistic Christian community and represents no more than a preliminary attempt to explain the divine sonship of Jesus. By contrast, argues Pannenberg, 'the traditions of the resurrection, as well as that of Jesus' empty tomb, are of a completely different sort: (even) where they have undergone legendary influence, something historical has been expanded in a different way.' Besides, the virgin birth has nothing like the same significance for Christianity as the resurrection. Here, Pannenberg rests his case on a quotation from Paul Althaus: 'There has never been a message about the Christ that was not an Easter message, certainly, however, there can be witness to Christ and faith in Christ without the virgin birth.'[7] He might equally well have rested on St Paul: 'if Christ has not been raised, your faith is futile; you are still in your sins.' It is impossible to imagine a similar apostolic statement on the virgin birth.[8]

Pannenberg is also sharply critical of Barth's portrayal of the virgin birth as a sign of the secret of the incarnation. To some extent, this is a continuation of his argument against historicity. If the virgin birth is mere legend then the sign is a mere human one, with no divine legitimacy. Unless it is first of all historical, it cannot be a sign. Conversely, however, if the virgin birth is (as Barth believes) historical, then it is also, like all miracles, a sign: a notable part of the process by which God attested Jesus by 'miracles, wonders and signs' (Acts 2: 22). In this connection, the comparison with John 1:13 is instructive. If the exclusion of human will and initiative from the new birth is a sign of the total sovereignty of grace, so the exclusion of human will from the birth of Jesus was a sign that the human race was not able to produce its own Saviour or to initiate its own salvation.

But Pannenberg's criticism also extends to the details of Barth's argument, in particular to the idea that Mary's virginity is the negation of man before God: a sign that man has no capacity for God. Here, Pannenberg argues, Barth is moving along the line of Mariological thought, deducing from the mere elimination of the male that woman has the greater capacity for God. In Pannenberg's view there is no warrant for this: 'in no case can it be asserted that the path of divine grace in actual history was, so to say, shorter to woman than to man' (*(Jesus*, 148). It is doubtful whether this is fair to Barth, who does not portray Mary as in any sense a meritorious contributor to the incarnation. She does not volunteer, or even, strictly speaking, consent. She is pregnant before she knows it and simply resigns herself to the *de facto* situation. On the other hand, Pannenberg is correct to point out that even a totally passive role (letting herself be acted on) could no more be sinless than an active one. Human beings lie under God's judgement on sin 'no less in their receptivity than in their creative activity' (*Jesus,* 148).

Is the virgin birth an alternative to the idea of the pre-existence of Jesus? Pannenberg certainly thinks so. Whereas in St Paul Jesus is the eternal, co-equal Son sent into the world on a mission of redemption, in the birth narratives of Matthew and Luke he is the Son of God only by virtue of his birth from the virgin (*The Apostles' Creed*, 63). The whole point of these narratives is that Jesus had no father apart from God. Pannenberg does not believe that the idea of the pre-existent sonship arose out of the story of the virgin birth. On the contrary, the story was an 'aetiological legend' developed to explain the title 'the Son of God', which had already been conferred for other reasons. Unfortunately, according to Pannenberg, the legend contradicts what came to be the primary explanation of Jesus' sonship: the doctrine of the incarnation. 'If Jesus,' he writes, 'was God's Son in that he was created in Mary by God, then he could not be already God's Son before, in the sense of pre-existence' (*The Apostles' Creed,* 76).

But it is difficult, surely, to see how anything in the birth narratives contradicts the idea of pre-existence. The humanity of

Jesus must have had a point of origin somewhere. It was certainly not pre-existent. It is that origin that is described in the accounts of the virgin birth, an idea which is totally compatible with both the idea of pre-existence and the idea of incarnation. This is not to say that the virgin birth is proposed either in the birth narratives or anywhere else in the New Testament as a rationale of incarnation (or even of sinlessness). Nor is it to say that the incarnation required a virgin birth. But it certainly required a supernatural one. The very fact that he was pre-existent and that therefore his birth could not mark the beginning of his existence seems by itself to demand something extraordinary. Besides, a child born in the normal way from two human parents would have been an independent person in his own right and any union between him/her and the eternal Son of God would have involved either Adoptionism or Nestorianism (and probably both).The argument that the rest of the New Testament knows nothing of the virgin birth requires to be treated with caution, but if the incarnation is to be described as a 'becoming' (with St John) or as an 'assumption' (with St Paul) the idea of a supernatural birth accords perfectly well with such wording.

On the other hand, the language used with regard to Jesus' humanity is extremely careful. There is no suggestion of any kind of physical relationship between God the Father and the virgin mother. Indeed, the Father's role is not even prominent. It is the activity of the Holy Spirit that is emphasised (Matt.1:18, 20, Luke 1:35). The exclusion of human paternity does not by itself explain the birth of Jesus. It merely creates space for the work of the Holy Spirit, who 'overshadows' the virgin (Luke 1:35).

Yet Jesus is never called the Son of the Holy Spirit. Nor in the Matthaean birth narrative is he even once referred to as the Son of God. He is Mary's Son (Matt. 1:21, 22, 25), he is given the name 'Jesus' because his calling is to be the Saviour and he is described (in a quotation from Isaiah 7:14) as 'Immanuel' because he is 'God with us'. Neither of these names is linked to divine paternity or to the Virgin Birth.

In the Lucan narrative Jesus is actually referred to as both the Son of the Most High and the Son of God. Equally clearly, however, he is referred to as the Son of Mary and, by implication, as the Son of David. In Luke 1:35, his divine sonship is directly linked to the circumstances of his birth: 'The Holy Spirit will come upon you, and the power of the Most High will overshadow you; therefore the child to be born will be called holy, the Son of God' (RSV). Even here, however, the link is not with God the Father, but with the Spirit. He is God's Son, first, in the negative sense that he is not Joseph's and, secondly, in the positive sense that on the human level, no less than on the divine, he is 'of God'. Far from ruling out a prior sonship, it could be argued, as we have seen, that it was exactly this prior sonship which made necessary a supernatural birth.

The resurrection
But if Pannenberg dismisses the virgin birth as legend his attitude to the resurrection is in total contrast. Here is a historical event, which left Jesus' tomb empty and made it possible for him to be seen by his disciples.

This confidence in 'the facticity of the resurrection of Jesus as the Christian faith proclaims it' (*Jesus*, 352) rests, according to Pannenberg, on three considerations.

First, the resurrection appearances. Pannenberg has considerably less confidence in the Synoptic accounts of these than he has in the Pauline, but he remains assured that behind all the accounts lies a historical core. These appearances were visual, but they were not in the psychological sense 'visionary'. Visions in that sense require a psychiatric point of contact which is totally lacking in the case of the disciples, who, prior to the appearances, were in no excited state. On the contrary, their faith had been shattered by the cross. Consequently, 'The Easter appearances are not to be explained from the Easter faith of the disciples; rather, conversely, the Easter faith of the disciples is to be explained from the appearances' (*Jesus,* 96).

The second reason for confidence in the historicity of the resurrection is the empty tomb. Pannenberg agrees that at first sight this is of less evidential value than the appearances since the emptiness of the tomb admits of more than one explanation. For example, it is possible, *a priori*, that the body was stolen. Nevertheless, the empty tomb, he argues, is a *sine qua non* of the resurrection: 'a self-evident implication of what was said about the resurrection of Jesus' (*Systematic Theology*, Vol. 2, 359) He quotes, again, from Paul Althaus, this time to the effect that the resurrection kerygma 'could not have been maintained in Jerusalem for a single day, for a single hour, if the emptiness of the tomb had not been established as a fact for all concerned' (*Jesus*, 100). He also argues (*Jesus*, 101) from 'the fact that the early Jewish polemic against the Christian message about Jesus' resurrection, traces of which have already been left in the Gospels, does not offer any suggestion that Jesus' grave had remained untouched. The Jewish polemic would have had to have every interest in the preservation of such a report. However, quite to the contrary, it shared the conviction with its Christian opponents that Jesus' grave was empty.'[9]

But the empty tomb is not significant merely as a self-evident adjunct to the resurrection. It also has significance for the event itself. For example, 'It creates difficulty for the theory that the appearances of the risen Lord might have been mere hallucinations' (*Systematic Theology*, Vol. 2, 359). It also tells against any superficial spiritualising of the Easter message. Easter faith by itself could not have emptied the tomb. Neither could hallucinations. The emptiness reinforces the belief that what was seen was the real Jesus. It also implies time-and-space historicity. If the resurrection were *super-history* it would not involve an empty tomb: 'the event took place in this world, namely, in the tomb of Jesus in Jerusalem before the visit of the women on the Sunday morning after his death' (*Systematic Theology*, Vol. 2, 360).

The third reason for confidence in the facticity of the resurrection, according to Pannenberg, is that it is an indispensable link in the chain of historical events which explains the origin of Christianity. Christianity itself is a historical fact and as such it involves certain other facts: the resurrection message of the early church, the worship of Jesus, the writing of the Gospels, the emergence and development of Christology and the disciples' belief that they had seen the risen Jesus. This body of facts does not explain itself. It requires another fact, equally historical, to explain it. That, argues Pannenberg, can be no other than the resurrection: 'it was only through the resurrection that it was possible to believe in him again at all after his death on the cross' (*The Apostles' Creed*, 53). Consequently, the resurrection was, 'historically speaking, the point of departure for the history of Christendom' (*The Apostles' Creed*, 96).[10] Without it, faith in this man who had experienced rejection and suffered crucifixion would have been impossible.

Pannenberg is obviously aware of the relativism of historical judgements and his language clearly reflects this. 'Assertion of the historicity of an event,' he writes, 'does not mean that its facticity is so sure that there can no longer be any dispute regarding it. Many statements of historical fact are actually debateable' (*Systematic Theology*, Vol. 2, 360). Such relativism is not confined to the resurrection, as Pannenberg makes clear in the every same paragraph: 'In principle, doubts may exist regarding all such statements.' The caution bred by such relativism is reflected in the guarded language Pannenberg uses to express his conclusion: 'It is perfectly possible to arrive at the opinion that, when one has subjected the early Christian traditions of Jesus' resurrection to a critical examination, the description of the event in the language of the eschatological hope still proves itself to be the most plausible, in the face of all rival explanations' (*The Apostles' Creed*, 113). Such language concedes too much to historical scepticism. However impossible it may be for 20th century scholars to achieve certainty on events which took place 2000 years ago it was not impossible for those who lived through the events themselves. They were able to check things out; and as Luke makes clear in the preface to his Gospel this is exactly what they did (Luke 1:1-4). Conversely, their contemporaries were in a position to falsify their claims. We are not. The modern historian is not only in a worse position than the first century believer. He is in a worse position than the first-century sceptic. The time for rebuttal is past.

Yet for all his deferential nodding in the direction of historical relativism, Pannenberg is not prepared to suspend judgement on the question of the resurrection. To do so would be to abandon all hope of giving a coherent account of Christian origins. 'If we ask about the origins of Christianity,' he writes, 'not merely in the sense of enquiring what the first Christians believed, but in the sense of a present-day evaluation of what was really at the bottom of the story which started Christianity off, then we have to face up to the problem of the Easter events' (*The Apostles' Creed,* 113).

At the same time he is acutely aware that the modern, 'scientific' concept of reality presents an almost insuperable barrier to belief in a historical resurrection. Twentieth-century man thinks it impossible that a resurrection of the dead could take place in any circumstances. But, Pannenberg argues, biblical culture saw reality not as a closed circle but as 'a field of divine action' (*Systematic Theology,* Vol. 2, 362). In any case, it is not the task of the historian to decide what is possible. His task is to evaluate facts. In this particular instance, rather than allow our view of reality to determine our attitude to the resurrection we must allow the resurrection to modify our view of reality.

For Pannenberg the resurrection constitutes the very core of his 'Christology from below'. It is this that distinguishes him, at least in his own view, not only from 'Christologies from above', but also from other 'Christologies from below'.[11] He views the resurrection as part of 'below': part of the earthly history of Jesus. It is as such that it is the basis of our perception of his divinity. We move from it to the belief that in Jesus we meet God.

Yet it can be questioned whether this is really a Christology 'from below' at all. Is it not a Christology which takes the resurrection as its starting-point and therefore views everything from above?

But Pannenberg does not begin with the resurrection: at least, not professedly. He begins with the New Testament data, treating these data not as canonical but as ordinary public, historical records, moves from these records to the resurrection and then moves from the resurrection to affirming Jesus' deity. In such a procedure, the resurrection is a 'below' event: as much so, for example, as the crucifixion.

But would Pannenberg ever have chosen this route were he

not starting from above in the first place. Psychologically, a believer cannot start from below. On this, we had better not delude ourselves.

What, then, is the precise function of the resurrection? Pannenberg first makes the point that only through the resurrection was it possible to believe in Jesus at all. The cross, on the face of things, falsified all Jesus' claims and invalidated all his work. 'Without the resurrection,' he writes, 'the apostles would have had no missionary message, nor would there have been any Christology relating to the person of Jesus' (*Systematic Theology,* Vol. 2, p.54).[12]

Secondly, the resurrection was, 'The Justification of Jesus by the Father' (*Systematic Theology,* Vol. 2, 343). This blanket-statement involves several key elements.

At the most fundamental level, the resurrection was a vindication of Jesus' expectations. These expectations were frankly apocalyptic, and Pannenberg is at pains to to stress that they were by no means peripheral to Jesus' message. They lay at its very centre: 'it is self-deception to think that one can separate the real heart of Jesus' message from his expectation of the imminent coming of the rule of God as the impending transformation of the world' (*The Apostles' Creed,* 52).

But 'has not Jesus' expectation already been refuted, in as much as the end of the world, far from having broken in on Jesus' own generation, has not taken place at all?' (*Creed,* 52).

No! according to Pannenberg: not if we take the resurrection seriously. If we do, we can no longer say that Jesus was mistaken. On the contrary, we can maintain that 'although Jesus' expectation of the imminent end of the world was certainly not fulfilled in the world as a whole, it was certainly fulfilled in his own person' (*Creed,*53).This means that in the risen Jesus the end of the world has already begun (*Jesus,* 67) and the universal resurrection has, in principle, already taken place. This in turn is a divine confirmation, first, that Jesus spoke the truth when he proclaimed the nearness of the kingdom and, secondly, that he himself was the bearer and inaugurator of that kingdom. He completely fulfilled the Jewish hope, in which the idea of the resurrection has its roots and from which the Easter message derived its linguistic expression and its conceptual framework.

It has been suggested, however, that this argument is valid only if we accept the 'horizon of the apocalyptic expectation' of later Judaism. If we do not, we have to reject the whole thesis and admit that we cannot see God's revelation in Jesus.

The problem is discussed briefly in Maurice Wiles' *Working Papers in Doctrine*.[13] Wiles believes, against Pannenberg's critics, that he is correct in asserting that we can ascribe absolute significance and *full*[14] divinity to Jesus only if we accept the apocalyptic context, including the idea of the immediate and dramatic culmination of all history. On the other hand, Wiles argues, if we reject such a context (as he believes we must) this would not necessarily mean that 'we had to abandon all perception whatsoever of God's revelation in Jesus'. It would mean only that we had to abandon our traditional forms of expression. We could no longer speak of Jesus in terms of substantial divinity. Nor could we speak of him as the world's one and only objective Saviour.

It is extremely doubtful, however, whether we could continue to regard Jesus as in any sense the revelation of God if we had to reject the apocalyptic framework of his message. The apocalyptic element, as we saw, was central. It involved a unique understanding of himself, of his mission, of the human condition and of the purposes of God. If he was wrong here, it is difficult to rescue anything of his 'revelation', apart from those elements of human insight common to all sages from Confucius to the *Sun*.

We may nevertheless question whether the role of Jesus as fulfiller of apocalyptic expectation is as decisive for New Testament Christology as Pannenberg suggests. As Richard Bauckham has pointed out, what the New Testament presents is a Christology of *divine identity*. It is not interested primarily in *what* Jesus is (a Christology of substance) nor in what Jesus *does* (a Christology of function). It is interested in *who* he is; and its answer to that is that he is God: a figure clearly distinguished from all creatures and also from all intermediate beings. To say that Jesus is God is to say that he is the one identified in Genesis as the Creator of the universe, the one who made a covenant with

Abraham, the one who delivered Israel at the exodus and the one who gave himself the special redemptive-historical name, Jahweh.[15]

It is difficult to see how the resurrection by itself can sustain such a Christology. It could do so only if the question, Who is God? were to be answered by saying, 'God is one who rises from the dead.' This, of course, is not the case. Pannenberg is correct to argue that belief in the divinity of Jesus must be historically grounded: that is, justified (though not compelled) by the facts ascertainable from the public records. This was true even of belief in the divinity of Jahweh himself. It was empirical in the sense that it was produced by Israel's experience of God's involvement and God's commitment. As far as Jesus is concerned, the core historical fact is his own self-consciousness: Who did he think he was? And were the circumstances and events of his life, taken as a whole, in keeping with who he thought he was? Pannenberg, because of his sceptical approach to the synoptic tradition has cut himself off from such an approach. He cannot accept that Jesus called himself the Messiah, or that by calling himself 'the Son of God' He was making a claim of any particular significance.[16] Yet the historicity of Jesus' use of such titles is as well substantiated as the resurrection; equally indispensable to understanding the origin and life of the early church, particularly its worship of Jesus; and virtually indispensable to understanding how a worship apparently so subversive of monotheism could so easily take hold in a Jewish matrix. When the early church acknowledged Jesus as God they acknowledged him not as Another God, but as *God*; as Jahweh, the God of Abraham, Isaac and Jacob.

We have to remember, too, that however important the resurrection, the roots of this worship lay in the disciples' pre-Easter experience. Indeed, it is surely significant that with the exception of Saul of Tarsus all the resurrection appearances were made to people who were already believers. For men such as Peter, the resurrection was not the birth of their hope, but its re-birth (1 Pet.1:3).

Yet we cannot allow that the resurrection of Jesus has no more significance, intrinsically, than the resurrection of Lazarus or of

Jairus' daughter. It is simplistic to argue that if resurrection in these instances did not prove divinity no more did it do so in the case of Jesus.[17] Pannenberg has fully covered this. The resurrection of Jesus is not the resurrection of just any man. It is the resurrection of *this* man. What matters here, according to Pannenberg, is not the goodness of Jesus, but precisely the opposite. To a Jew, the claims of the pre-Easter Jesus were blasphemous. This was why they had him crucified; and the crucifixion itself would have been seen as a definitive word of divine judgement. Against this background, the resurrection was a vindication of Jesus by the very God whom he had allegedly blasphemed: a dramatic reversal of both the popular condemnation and the apparent divine retribution.

Resurrection as metaphor
So far, we have assumed that Pannenberg's views on the historicity of the resurrection can be taken at face-value: he believes that the resurrection was a real event: a factual *resurrectio carnis*. But things may not be quite as they appear. G E Michalson, for example, has argued that whereas, to begin with, Pannenberg seems to be seeking to prove that the resurrection was a physical event involving the resuscitation or re-animation of the body of Jesus, in the end he distances himself completely from such a concept. 'It turns out,' he writes, 'that he has *no intention* of defending the notion that the corpse of Christ was resuscitated.... Instead, the term resurrection is to be understood as a "metaphor".'[18] Accordingly, Michalson argues, Pannenberg ends up affirming what he expressly set out to deny, namely, that the resurrection is about the experiences of the first Christians, not about the object of their experience. For him, as for the post-Enlightenment theology from which he seemed to be distancing himself, *what* the first Christians experienced is not accessible to historical research.

It is certainly true that Pannenberg repeatedly uses the word *metaphor* in connection with the resurrection. He does so, for example, in his *Systematic Theology:* 'The language of the resurrection of Jesus is that of metaphor' (Vol. 2, 346).[19] As such, it rests on the underlying metaphor which speaks of death as sleep. This is part of the reason that Pannenberg prefers Paul's account of the resurrection appearances (1 Cor. 15:5-7) to the Synoptists': the latter have a tendency 'to underscore the corporeality of the encounters' and therefore 'offer no firm basis for historical considerations' (*Jesus*, 92). He further denies that the resurrection was a return to earthly life and describes it instead as a 'transition to the new eschatological life' (*Systematic Theology*, Vol. 2, 348). He is therefore at pains to distinguish the personal resurrection of Jesus from the resurrection-miracles performed in the cases of Lazarus, the young man from Nain and Jairus' daughter. These were mere resuscitations: the restoring of life to corpses. Jesus' resurrection was on an altogether different plane. It was a radical transformation. This is clear, he argues, from Paul's account of his experience of the risen Jesus. What he saw could not be confused with a resuscitated corpse: 'it confronted him as a reality of an entirely different sort' (*Jesus,* 77). It was no mere return to life as we know it, 'but a transformation into an entirely new life' (*The Apostles' Creed*, 97). On the question what precisely is meant by this new life Pannenberg, like the rest of us, must remain agnostic. He has to resort to the *via negativa:* it is 'an immortal life no longer bounded by any death, which must therefore be in any case different from the form of life of organisms known to us' (*The Apostles' Creed,* 100). The transformation is so radical that nothing remains unchanged.

Other indications in Pannenberg point, however, in a different direction and seem quite incompatible with a merely 'spiritual' resurrection.[20] For example, despite his reliance on Paul's description of the resurrection body as 'spiritual' (*pneumatikon*, 1 Cor. 15:44), he explicitly repudiates the view that this points to 'a disembodied spirituality, in the sense of some Platonic tradition or other'. Instead, he takes the position that 'in Paul's sense God's "Spirit" is the creative origin of all life, and a spiritual body is a living being which, instead of being separated from this origin – as we are in our present existence – remains united with it; so that it is a life which no death can end any more' (*The Apostles' Creed,* 98-99). It is also important to note Pannenberg's stress on the empty tomb, which, as he says, rules out any superficial spirituality of the Easter message (*Systematic Theology,* Vol. 1, 359). No merely 'spiritual' resurrection (and certainly no resurrection 'occurring' only in the minds of the disciples) could have resulted in the disappearance of Jesus' body from its burial place.

Above all, Pannenberg stresses that it is Jesus himself who was the subject of the resurrection. His thesis is 'that Jesus rose again, that the dead Jesus of Nazareth came to a new life' (*Systematic Theology,* Vol. 2, 359). This involves an explicit repudiation of the idea that the change took place only in the minds of the disciples; and an equally explicit repudiation of the idea that the early kerygma announced merely 'that something took place that transcends human history in space and time' (*Systematic Theology,* Vol. 2, 360).[21] On the contrary, the resurrection was an 'event' which occurred at a specific time and at a particular place.

We should be careful, too, about drawing hasty conclusions from Pannenberg's use of the idea of metaphor in connection with the resurrection. It is one thing to suggest that the resurrection itself is a mere metaphor (a figure of speech for something else) and quite another to suggest that *language* about the resurrection (and even the word *resurrection* itself) is metaphorical. It is the latter course that Pannenberg is taking and (as he is careful to point out) the metaphorical nature of the language 'comes directly from the inner logic of the concept itself' (*Jesus,* 74). In rests, as we have seen, on a prior metaphor: the comparison of death to sleep. *We* rise from sleep. *Jesus* rose from death. From this point of view, to describe the language of the resurrection as metaphorical no more denies the reality of the event itself than the New Testament description of believers as 'sleeping' (for example, in 1 Thess. 4:13) denies the reality of their deaths. Many New Testament concepts are defined in metaphorical language. Christian initiation, for example, is described in a variety of terms, all of them metaphorical: conversion, regeneration and new birth, to name but a few. To recognise the metaphorical nature of such language is not to deny the reality of the experience. Similarly, if Pannenberg argues that the New Testament uses metaphorical language to explain the post-crucifixion appearances of Jesus this in no way undermines the central point that the appearances themselves were real. Pannenberg points out, for example, that the references to resurrection in Jewish apocalyptic works were metaphorical: 'Yet in spite of the metaphorical language, a real event was in view, as also in the case of the resurrection of Jesus' (*Systematic Theology,* Vol. 2, 346).

Christology cannot escape from metaphorical language, whether these metaphors be spatial (advent, ascension), political (king, servant) or ceremonial (coronation, anointing). What matters is that the metaphor points to reality. I do not deny a man's existence by calling him a brick.

In the last analysis we have to accept, with Pannenberg, that however real the resurrection it was not merely a return to life as we know it. He is quite correct to distinguish it from the resuscitation of corpses sometimes alluded to in ancient literature and even from the resuscitations accomplished by Jesus himself in the course of his earthly ministry (*Jesus,* 77). These were merely temporary restorations to the old life and all who experienced them subsequently died. Jesus' resurrection was completely different. He rose to a permanent life of absolute immortality. Death has no more dominion over him (Rom. 6:9)

The New Testament data on the resurrection body of Jesus are extraordinarily complex. It would be hazardous, therefore, to read too much into the language of Luke 24:39, 'a ghost does not have flesh and bones as you see I have.' The risen Jesus was certainly no mere apparition. But then neither need he have had the exact same biochemistry as you and I. The same caution should be applied to Luke 24:42. The fact that Jesus ate the fish no more proves that his corporeality was identical with ours than the fact that Abraham's Three Visitors shared a meal with him (Gen. 18:18) proves they were not angels.

There are two points of special interest.

First, in the period between his resurrection and ascension Jesus' appearance, according to the Gospels, showed remarkable variations. Mary (John 20:15) mistook him for a gardener. The disciples in the Upper Room recognised him instantly. The travellers on the road to Emmaus did not recognise him at all.

Mark (admittedly in the Longer Ending) explicitly states that he appeared to two disciples 'in a different form' (Mark16:12). No ordinary body would have been capable of such variation.

Secondly, descriptions of the post-Ascension Jesus portray a Christ radically different from both the pre-crucifixion Jesus and the Jesus of the resurrection appearances. Paul could never have mistaken the Christ of the Damascus Road for a gardener. Neither could John in Patmos (Rev. 1:12-20) have imagined that what he was seeing was a ghost, far less a resuscitated corpse. Paradoxically, however, these two descriptions accord perfectly with the account of the Transfiguration, which was surely, at one level, a proleptic disclosure of the glory of the risen saviour.

It is clear that the risen Christ is a transfigured Christ. That is not to deny his corporeality. It is only to say that his corporeality, now, is of a different order from ours. It belongs to the age to come: to the new heavens and the new earth (2 Pet. 3:13). In this respect Pannenberg is absolutely right to portray Christ as the revelation in history of the consummation of history. In him, man (and indeed the whole of created reality) have already reached their Omega-point. His is a body whose glory now accords fully with the divine glory in which it shares. That immediately creates a discontinuity with our present corporeality. Yet we, in him and even now, share in the divine nature (2 Pet. 1:4); and in the moment of resurrection we shall receive a corporeality as glorious as his.[22]

The mode of God's presence in Jesus

But, granting the historicity of the resurrection, what, exactly, does it illuminate? What is the nature of Jesus' relationship to God? Pannenberg devotes a substantial section of *Jesus: God and Man* to the question of the Mode of God's Presence in Jesus, beginning with a brief survey of the various formulations proposed in the patristic period. One of the earliest of these was the attempt to define God's presence by means of the Spirit. This took its cue from the close relation between Jesus and the Spirit indicated by the New Testament itself. It appears for example in the 'double movement' or 'two-stage Christology' of Romans 1:3f., which speaks of Jesus 'according to the flesh' and 'according to the

Spirit'. It also appears in accounts of Jesus' baptism (Mark 1:9-11 and parallels). Clearly, then, Jesus was a bearer of the Spirit. But later Adoptionism (as represented first by Theodotus the Tanner and subsequently by Paul of Samosata) went a stage further and argued that this was the only way in which he was the Son of God. He was a Spirit-filled man who differed from Moses and the prophets only in degree. In the event, however, Pannenberg's treatment of Adoptionism is left hanging in the air. He refrains from any clear critique.[23]

Pannenberg also rushes through three other options: Substantial Presence, Mediation Christology and Presence as Appearance. He recognises that the first was the dominant understanding in patristic Christology (mainly because it was adopted by Nicea), but does little more than define it: 'According to this, God himself is fully and completely present in Jesus; Jesus Christ is not a mere man, but a divine person' (*Jesus*, 121).

Mediator Christologies are those which discount any substantial presence of God in Jesus and portray him instead as a median being who 'is subordinated to God, but stands higher than man' (*Jesus*, 123). The early church, argues Pannenberg, rejected this for soteriological reasons: 'we can have full community with God through Christ, we can have deification, only if he is God in the fullest sense' (*Jesus*, 124). This is true, of course, but it is not the whole truth and perhaps not even the most important truth. There were also powerful liturgical reasons for rejecting Arianism, the most important form of Mediator Christology. To worship a creature, however exalted, would have been pure paganism. Christian worship required a Christology of divine identity.

Pannenberg also dismisses the idea of Presence as Appearance; or, as he expresses it more precisely, 'an epiphany of God or of a divine being without, however, accepting as a consequence an identity in essence of this with Jesus' (*Jesus*, 125). The prime example of this was Gnosticism, but it also found expression in the Modalism of Sabellius, who denied the presence in Jesus of a particular divine hypostasis distinct from the Father and portrayed Him instead as 'a particular mode of the efficacy of the one deity in saving history' (*Jesus*, 126). On this view, Creator, Saviour and Spirit are not distinct 'persons' within the godhead, but successive phases of the divine activity. But here again Pannenberg contents himself with summary and offers little by way of critique.

The reason for the almost impatient treatment of these four approaches is that Pannenberg wants to propose a fifth: a *Revelational* Presence of God in Christ. This, he claims, is the only appropriate understanding of the presence of God in Jesus. At the same time he is at pains to point out that the idea of revelatory presence is not to be seen as an alternative to identity of essence. Instead, it includes 'the idea of substantial presence, of an essential identity of Jesus with God' *((Jesus*, 127). Appearance and essence belong together. This rests, as far as Pannenberg is concerned, on what he calls the 'modern' understanding of revelation as *self*-revelation. It is not the communication of religious truths by supernatural means, but God's self-disclosure. This includes the idea that the Revealer and what is revealed (the Revelation) are identical. If, then, Christ is the revelation of God he can only be the *self*-revelation of God; and if he is the self-revelation of God he must be the *self* who is revealed: 'Thus to speak of a self-revelation of God in the Christ event means that the Christ event, that Jesus, belongs to the essence of God himself.... Then Jesus belongs to the definition of God and thus to his divinity, to his essence' *(Jesus*, 129f.).

From an evangelical perspective this stress on the essential divinity of Jesus is welcome. But Pannenberg's approach still raises serious problems. For one thing, in biblical thought the self-revelation of God is not confined to Jesus. As the Writer to the Hebrews points out, revelation took place at different times and in different ways (Heb. 1:1) and this remains true no matter how firmly we may wish to emphasis the uniqueness of Christ as the exclusive way to God. Does it follow, then, that all prophets and apostles were also revelations, identical in essence with God? If not, how, in the case of Jesus, are we to make the leap from revealer to revelation and from revelation to revealed-one?

The answer, according to Pannneberg, is, inevitably, the resurrection. This proves that Jesus was the revelation of God (part of the definition of God) not only from the resurrection

onwards but from the beginning of his life on earth and even from
eternity itself. It does so because it is a vindication of his earthly
life and ministry: despite having made the apparently blasphemous
claim that he himself was the kingdom and despite suffering the
fate appropriate to such blasphemy God vindicated him; and this
could be nothing else than his vindication as the self-revelation of
God.

But from Pannenberg's chosen stand-point this is highly
problematical. The earthly life vindicated in the resurrection was
purely human. Jesus had no consciousness of being divine and
never defined himself as divine. He never, for example, claimed
to be the Son of God, the Son of Man or even the Messiah. In fact,
in classical Liberal fashion Pannenberg repeatedly insists that the
message of the pre-Easter Jesus (unlike that of the post-Easter
church) was not about himself at all. How then could the
resurrection be about himself?

Pannenberg's answer is that it is precisely in making no claims
for himself that Jesus is God. But this requires us to believe that
the defining characteristic of God (what identifies him as the one
he, uniquely, is) is that he is the one who makes no claims for
himself. In fact this leads to a fundamental cleavage within the
deity. As the Father, God is the one who requires submission. As
the Son, God is the one who renders submission. Is this simply
God being God in two different ways? Or is it a pointer to two
incompatible deities?

Pannenberg's overriding concern is to build up his Christology
from below: to move from the earthly, historical Jesus to the
modern theologian's final synthesis, *Jesus: God and Man. A priori*,
this would suggest a determination to start with the public records
(the Gospels), create from these a picture of the historical Jesus
and then use that picture as the core element in Christology. But
what Pannenberg delivers is nothing like that. Had he really taken
a route through the Gospels it would surely have dawned on him
that far from deducing his identity from the fact of his being the
revelation of God the New Testament has an exactly opposite
approach: it treats Jesus as the revelation of God because of his
divine identity. Nor is this a matter merely of the post-Easter

kerygma. According to the Gospels (our only public records) the pre-Easter Jesus was conscious of authority to forgive sins, to legislate for the Sabbath and to set aside tradition. He even claimed (on the specific basis of his divine sonship) that the very things which had been hidden from the wise and prudent had been revealed to him (Matt.11:25). Pannenberg's answer is that none of this material is historical. The story of the baptism, not less than the virgin birth, is legendary (*Jesus,* 139). So, too, is everything else that might suggest any pre-Easter consciousness of deity on Jesus' part.

It seems to me that this leaves Pannenberg in a hopeless position. How can the resurrection narratives be the sole survivors of the solvents of biblical criticism? How can we argue that the stories of the appearances are history while all around them is myth and legend? More fundamentally, how can there be a Christology 'from below' if we have no reliable records of Jesus' life 'below'? Pannenberg is building up his Christology not from the public records (part of 'universal history') but from the abstract truth of Jesus' humanity. But what progress is possible when all we know is that he was a man and when we know nothing of the kind of man he was?

On the other hand, were Pannenberg to take the records seriously rather than selectively he would find that they are inconsistent with the whole tendency of his thought. In them, the presumption that Jesus is divine comes before the perception that he is the revelation of God. This is true not only of his disciples, but of himself. The Christ of the records can offer to teach all the illiterate and to relieve all the oppressed precisely because he is the Son of God (Matt.11.28, 29).

The incarnation

Does Pannenberg, then, believe in the incarnation? He certainly thinks he does, and much of his language accords with it. He clearly affirms his belief in the deity of Christ (*Systematic Theology,* Vol. 1, Chapter 10) and his whole discussion of the question of the unity of Jesus with God presupposes the incarnation (*Jesus,* 133-158). He also believes, in some sense, in the pre-existence of Christ, which, he thinks, follows from the revelatory presence of God in Jesus. 'If,' he writes, 'the relation of the historical person of Jesus of Nazareth in eternity characterises the identity of God as Father, then we must speak of a pre-existence of the Son, who was historically manifested in Jesus of Nazareth, even before his earthly birth. Then we also must view the earthly existence of Jesus as the event of the incarnation of the pre-existent Son' (*Systematic Theology*, Vol. 1, 368).

Yet Brian Hebblethwaite can write, 'Wolfhart Pannenberg only retains an incarnational Christology by the skin of his teeth'; and Colin Gunton can even say, 'Pannenberg belongs in the tradition of liberal and Kantian Christology.'[24]

There are two main problems.

First, Pannenberg's definition of the deity of Jesus. He insists that it is as man that he is God. That, of course, can bear a perfectly orthodox meaning, but when he asks, 'In what sense is Jesus God?' he comes perilously close to answering that his manhood *is* his deity.[25] Part of the paradox of Pannenberg's 'Christology from below' is that he dispenses with the Christ of the Gospels and takes as his 'below' the Christ of historical research. This Christ, as we have seen, never used divine titles, never made divine claims and never asserted his equality with God. But far from being a problem, this, according to Pannenberg, is the very core of his deity. Had he not avoided making himself equal with God, Christian faith could not recognise his sonship. He makes this plain in a crucially important passage: 'For Christian faith much depends on whether Jesus avoided making himself equal with God. That is, it depends on whether, as a creature of God, he subordinated himself to the imminent rule of God that he announced with just the same unconditionality as he required of others. Only in this subordination to the rule of the one God is he the Son. As he gave his life in service to the rule of God over his creatures – namely, to prepare the way for its acknowledgement – he is as man the Son of the eternal Father. *Rejection of any supracreaturely dignity before God shows itself to be a condition of his sonship.*'[26]

Part of the meaning of this is that Jesus' divine sonship is 'indirect'. It is not a relationship between his human nature and his divine or between his human nature and the Logos. Neither of these statements gives any difficulty. But when Pannenberg goes on to limit the sonship to a relationship between the *man* Jesus and the Father and to state that it consists, exclusively, in his human, filial submission to the Father, things become more problematical. This submission climaxes on Calvary, seen, not in terms of traditional understandings of the atonement, but as the failure of Jesus' mission: 'only in the dedication to God's will in the darkness of his fate on the cross – which meant first of all the failure of his mission – did Jesus' dedication to God take on the character of self-sacrifice.... This relation of dedication to the point of self-sacrifice was the personal community of the man Jesus with the God of his message, the heavenly Father.'[27] It is precisely this that is confirmed in the resurrection. Jesus is the man who 'reserved nothing for himself in his human existence', but lived for God and for the men who must be called into his kingdom (*Jesus,* 335).

Hebblethwaite has described Pannenberg's thinking at this point as characterised by extreme difficulty and roundabout conceptuality:[28] something of an understatement. One result is that there must always be some doubt whether we have grasped his meaning. It does seem clear, however, that whenever Pannenberg speaks of the man Jesus as submitting to the will of God and even enduring failure as an act of self-sacrifice what he is really doing is stating his own ideal for humanity, reading that off into Jesus and then transforming it into a definition of deity. It is as the Ideal Man that he is divine, the Son of God. This justifies Runia's suggestion that Pannenberg's Christology 'from below' really issues in a deification of man.[29] Gunton makes a similar assessment, using different terminology. He classifies Pannenberg's position as 'degree Christology' and continues: 'We cannot then speak of the absolute uniqueness of Jesus, or of a uniqueness in kind: rather, we must teach that he differed from us only in degree.'[30]

This becomes all the more pronounced if we recall Pannenberg's understanding of the resurrection. At one level, it is the vindication and illustration of the deity of Jesus. At another, it is an anticipation of the end-time. The risen Christ is the end-point, from which alone history can be understood. In him, universal history has already achieved its goal, the future has already been revealed, the end of the world has begun and the resurrection of other men will immediately follow (*Jesus*, 67).[31] In the process the empty tomb has declared Jesus to be the definitive form of humanity, the eschatological man.

The question is, Will the general resurrection do for all of us what his personal resurrection did for Jesus? Will it declare each one of us to be definitive forms of humanity and thus vindicate and illustrate *our* divinity?

A second difficulty with Pannenberg's doctrine of the incarnation is that the man Jesus, when 'below', did not know that he was God. This explains why he never used divine titles and never even addressed God as 'Abba'. Indeed, had he, as man, taken such liberties and claimed equality with God this would have been blasphemy and clear proof in itself that he was no Son of God. Only in the light of the resurrection (proleptically, the moment when every knee bows and every tongue confesses that he is Lord) could he know his own deity.

The assumption behind such reasoning is that it would have been psychologically impossible for Jesus to live a truly human life if he had known he was God. Surely, however, this is taking us beyond what we can reasonably claim to know? How can our human wisdom pronounce on the psychological conditions of incarnation?

Besides, the argument can be reversed: how could Jesus be God (incarnate) and not know it? Pannenberg is rightly critical of 19th century Kenotic theories which argued that in laying aside the form of deity Christ divested himself of such divine attributes as omniscience. But is this not precisely what he himself is doing? Could there have been any greater eclipsing of divine omniscience than the spectacle of the Son of God moving about the streets of Jerusalem not knowing who he was? Memory and self-consciousness are essential components of personal identity. To deny them to Jesus is fatal to the idea of his being God incarnate. If he is God *as this man* (as Pannenberg holds) then, precisely *as this man* he knows that he is God. Indeed, this self-understanding is the only possible basis for a Christology 'from below'. That the early church believed him to be God is beyond dispute. But if that belief cannot be traced back beyond the kerygma to the self-understanding and self-disclosure of Jesus then history is fatal to the doctrine of the incarnation. It leaves a chasm between Jesus and the early church which no emphasis on the resurrection can overcome. According to the public records, recognition of Jesus' deity was already in place before Easter; and it was in place precisely because he had not concealed from his disciples his unique relation to God. Without such prior belief (and without Jesus' own predictions of his resurrection) there would have been no interpretative framework for news of the empty tomb. Had Jesus of Nazareth lived a totally non-notable life, characterised by no extraordinary deeds and marked by no unusual claims, the resurrection by itself could never have launched or sustained the idea of his being God incarnate. We cannot create a supernatural-free zone from Virgin Birth to Crucifixion and then suddenly introduce mega-miracle. It is only as the resurrection coheres with all that has gone before that it has any significance. It is the resurrection of *this* man.

We should note, too, that it is possible to put Pannenberg's argument from psychology to a use that he himself does not consider. If it is inconsistent with truly human activity and authentic human attributes to know that one is God, that must be as true of the post-Easter Jesus as of the pre-Easter one. The risen Christ is human. Yet, Pannenberg himself being judge, this cannot mean that Christ is unaware of his divine identity. He knows that he is the Son of God. This is a clear admission, is it not, that it is in fact possible for Jesus to be aware of his deity and yet to live an authentic human life, albeit a glorified one?

Conclusion

Pannenberg's work clearly raises important issues relating both to theological method and to the details of theological formulation. But it also raises, incidentally, serious questions as to the nature of the theological task itself: particularly the task of Christian theology. Pannenberg is heavy-going. Indeed, it is hard to avoid the impression that he glories in it.

This raises four specific questions.

First, is it not the responsibility of theologians to be elucidatory and expository? If so, then they should be more lucid and accessible than what they are trying to expound. Otherwise they are useless. What is the point of our Protestant doctrine of the perspicuity of Scripture if our expositions of it are impenetrable?

Secondly, is it not the duty of the theologian, as of any other author, to be interesting? If not, why should we expect people to read us?

Thirdly, is it not the duty of Christian theology to be ministerial: and in being ministerial to serve not merely one's fellow academics but the whole Christian community? It is hard to see how such work as Pannenberg's falls within the perspective of equipping the saints for ministry (Eph. 4:12).

Finally, is the theologian the one Christian functionary who is not bound by the example of Jesus? He was the Teacher *par excellence*. Sometimes, beyond a doubt, he uttered hard sayings. More often, his utterances aimed to tease the imagination and to fill the mind with ideas which no propositions could exhaust. But always, the concern was with people, with life and with practical wisdom *(hokmah)*.

It is a curious irony that modern theology, so critical of Scholasticism, now finds itself prisoner of its own schools.

References

1. W. Pannenberg, *Jesus – God and Man* (London: SCM Press, 1968). Translated from the German *Grundzuge der Christologie* (Gutersloher, 1964). Hereafter cited as *Jesus*.

2. W. Pannenberg, *The Apostles' Creed in the Light of Today's Questions* (London: SCM Press, 1972). From the German, *Das Glaubenbekenntis ausgelegt und verantwortet vor den Fragen der Gegenwart*, Hamburg, 1972). Hereafter cited as *The Apostles' Creed*.

3. W. Pannenberg, *Systematic Theology*, Volume 2, pp.277-396 (Grand Rapids: Eerdmans, 1994. From the German, *Systematische Theologie*, band 2, Gottingen, 1991).

4. For Barth, see *Church Dogmatics* (Edinburgh: T&T Clark, 12 vols, 1936-1962), Vol. IV, Part 1, Section 59 and Vol. IV, Part 2, Section 64. For Brunner, see *The Mediator* (London: Lutterworth Press, 1934), 201-327. Brunner, however, took a different approach in his *Dogmatics*. See Brunner, *The Christian Doctrine of Creation and Redemption* (London: Lutterworth Press, 1952), 322-378).

5. The text here is disputable, but the words *huiou theou* are well attested.

6. Compare *The Apostles' Creed*, 71-77; and *Systematic Theology*, Vol. 2, 315-319.

7. P. Althaus, *Die christliche Wahrheit*, 443 (quoted in *Jesus – God and Man*, 149).

8. I have looked more closely at the problems associated with the birth narratives in D. Macleod, *The Person of Christ* (Leicester: Inter-Varsity Press, 1998), 25-43.

9. Similar sentiments are expressed in *Systematic Theology*, Vol. 2, 357-358.

10. Cf. *Systematic Theology*, Vol. 2, 343-344: 'The resurrection of Jesus from the dead ... forms the starting-point of the apostolic proclamation of Christ and also of the history of the primitive Christian community. Without the resurrection the apostles would have had no missionary message, nor would there have been any Christology relating to the person of Jesus.'

11. See, for example, the statement in *Jesus – God and Man*, 108: 'The thesis presented in this paragraph that Jesus' resurrection is the basis for the perception of his divinity, that it means above all God's revelation in him, stands in contrast to the way in which a Christology "from below" is set up elsewhere in contemporary theological work.'

12. Cf. *The Apostles' Creed*, 54: 'only the Easter message can answer the challenge presented to the authority of Jesus by his crucifixion.'

13. M. Wiles, *Working Papers in Doctrine* (London: SCM Press, 1976), 160-161.

14. The italics are Wiles'.

15. See R. Bauckham, *God Crucified: Monotheism and Christology in the New Testament* (Carlisle: Paternoster Press, 1998). Bauckham is particularly concerned with the argument that the roots of New Testament Christology lie in the semi-divine figures allegedly prominent in Second Temple Judaism. See, for example, L. Hurtado, *One God, One Lord: Early Christian Devotion and Ancient Jewish Monotheism* (Second edition, Edinburgh, T&T Clark, 1998). Bauckham summarises his own position as follows: 'I shall argue that high Christology was possible within a Jewish monotheistic context, not by applying to Jesus a Jewish category of semi-divine intermediary status, but by identifying Jesus directly with the one God of Israel, including Jesus in the unique identity of this one God.' (page 4).

16. See, for example, *The Apostles' Creed*, 55-57, 61-65.

17. Cf. the comments of James P. Mackey in *Jesus: the Man and the Myth* (London: SCM Press, 1979), 92. Referring to the raising of Lazarus, he writes, 'Whether that story is to be taken as literally true or symbolic of something else, at least it clear that the writer who tells the story does not even consider that he has involved himself in the

kinds of claim to status and function in the case of Lazarus which are present in the case of the risen Jesus. Yet, and here is the question which must cause difficulty ... what could a witness to a raising from the dead see that would constitute a claim to have witnessed more than the revival of a dead man?'

18. From G. E. Michalson, 'Pannenberg on the Resurrection and Historical Method' in *Scottish Journal of Theology*, Vol. 33 No 4 (1980), 345-359.

19. Cf. *Jesus*, 75: 'To speak about the resurrection of the dead is not comparable to speaking about any random circumstance that can be identified empirically at any time. Here we are dealing, rather, with a metaphor.'

20. For a consistent spiritual/metaphorical understanding of the resurrection, see James P Mackey, *Jesus: the Man and the Myth,* 94-120. For example, commenting on Paul's argument in 1 Corinthians Fifteen, Mackey writes, 'It is highly unlikely, then, that Paul in this chapter understands the resurrection of Jesus primarily as an event of Jesus' own personal destiny.... It is much more likely, from both the wording and the logic of his argument here, that he understands by the resurrection of Jesus primarily the Christian experience of Jesus as Spirit or Lord in the lives of his followers.' (97). For the opposite point of view see Robert H. Gundry, 'The Essential Physicality of Jesus' Resurrection' in Joel B. Green and Max Turner (Eds.), *Jesus of Nazareth: Lord and Christ* (Carlisle: Paternoster Press, 1994), 204-219.

21. Cf. Pannenberg's explicit rejection of the view expressed by Karl Barth in the second and subsequent editions of his commentary, *The Epistle to the Romans* (ET, London: Oxford University Press, 1933, p.195) 'that the raising of Jesus from the dead is not an event in history elongated so as still to remain an event in the midst of other events. The Resurrection is the non-historical relating of the whole historical life of Jesus to its origin in God.' This, comments Pannenberg, is reminiscent of 'Bultmann's controversial thesis that Jesus' resurrection is only "The expression of the significance of the cross."'

22. See *Jesus: God and Man,* 111.

23. The question of the nature of the resurrection body has not received much attention. W. Milligan, *The Resurrection of our Lord* (London: Macmillan, 1890) is still worth consulting, especially pages 7-38.

24. Outside of his specific treatment of Adoptionism Pannenberg does express himself strongly, asserting that in contrast to 'the patristic idea of a substantial presence of God in Jesus' 'a mere presence of theSpirit remains just as inadequate as the mere presence of an appearnce of a being who is still to be distinguished from his appearance' (*Jesus*, 132).

25. B. Hebblethwaite, *The Incarnation* (Cambridge: Cambridge University Press, 1987), 155; C Gunton, *Yesterday and Today: a Study of Continuities in Christology* (London: 2nd edition, SPCK, 1997), 25.

26. Hence the remark of Gunton (*Yesterday and Today*, 22), 'Despite all his careful safeguards and detailed conversation with tradition, it is difficult to see how Pannenberg can avoid. an outcome similar to that of degree Christology, of making Jesus into a divinised man.'

27. *Systematic Theology,* Vol. 1, 273 (italics mine).

28. *Jesus: God and Man,* 335.

29. B. Hebblethwaite, *The Incarnation,* 155.

30. K. Runia, *The Present-day Christological Debate* (Leicester: Inter-Varsity Press, 1984), 38.

31. C. Gunton, *Yesterday and Today,* 15.

32. See further Alister McGrath's comments on Pannenberg's use of the apocalyptic world-view as a hermeneutical grid for interpreting the life, death and resurrection of

Jesus (article 'Pannenberg' in A. E. McGrath, Ed., *The Blackwell Encyclopaedia of Modern Christian Thought*, [Oxford: Blackwell, 1993], 420-422. Behind this lies Pannenberg's espousal of a neo- Hegelian philosophy of history (another of his life-long preoccupations). Cf. Gunton, *Yesterday and Today*, 28: 'Underlying all that Pannenberg writes is a view of the meaningfulness of universal history released, by anticipation, in the resurrection of Jesus of Nazareth.... Will the outcome be very much different from the reflection of the face of neo-Hegelian man in the well of universal history?' On the other hand, we should recognise the value of Pannenberg's stress on revelation as occurring in *history,* that is, in such publicly accessible events as the exodus and the resurrection.

SCRIPTURE INDEX

PERSONS INDEX

SUBJECT INDEX

Family Expositor 95
Fathers (of the Church) 89, 90, 98, 100, 125, 127, 146 *See also* Apostolic, Nicene, ante- *and* post-Nicene Fathers
feminism 145-6
German Liberalism 148
Gnostics 11, 16, 178
Hellenism 43
historical Jesus 116-19
Holy Spirit 93-4, 97-8,109-10, 124, 130, 132, 134, 136, 148, 154, 177
incarnation of Jesus 181-5
immutability 111-12
impassibility 153-5
incarnation 12, 27, 29, 41, 50-2, 70, 97, 107, 115-6, 124, 127, 129-32, 135, 137, 145, 151-2, 154, 156, 181-85
incarnational redemption 129-32
Israel 13, 18, 148, 149
Jews/Jewish 9, 16, 17, 26, 30, 43, 52-3, 74, 77, 94, 96, 146, 148-50, 159
Judaism 13, 61, 64, 149, 162, 171
judgment 39, 46, 50, 64, 66-8, 72, 75, 78-9, 117
kenosis 32, 34, 36-7, 51, 73, 111-12, 115-16, 125, 138-9, 155
kenoticism 111, 114-15, 124
krupsis 139
kurios 43-6, 48, 52-3
Last Adam Christology 30-38
Liberation Theology 157, 160
Lord's Prayer 150

Manicheism 110
Messiah 13, 26, 49, 69, 78, 84, 117, 148-50
messiahship 63, 68, 148-9
messianic advent 148
messianic hope 146, 148-9
messianic secret 58, 61, 83-4
modalism 178
mode of God's presence in Jesus, 177ff
monotheism 9, 13, 38, 53, 123
Nestorianism 110, 116, 128, 165
Nicaeno-Constantinopolitan Creed 87, 125
Nicea, Council of 88, 100,120
Nicene 115
Nicene Creed 87, 89, 100, 102, 120, 121, 149
Nicene Fathers 89, 120
Non-conformity 91-2
parousia 19, 62-4, 69, 72-4, 147, 150-2
passibility 155-6 *See also* suffering of God
passion (of Christ) 61-2, 64, 69, 72, 80, 152, 156
Patripassianism 124, 154
Patripassians 15
peace movement 145
political activism 145-6
polytheism 24
post-Nicene Fathers 98
pre-existence of Christ 28-34, 55, 69, 75, 94-7, 114-5, 124, 145
presbyterianism 121
presbyterians 91
promise (divine) 147-8, 151

Christian Focus Publications publishes biblically-accurate books for adults and children. The books in the adult range are published in three imprints.

Christian Heritage contains classic writings from the past.

Christian Focus contains popular works including biographies, commentaries, doctrine, and Christian living.

Mentor focuses on books written at a level suitable for Bible College and seminary students, pastors, and others; the imprint includes commentaries, doctrinal studies, examination of current issues, and church history.

For a free catalogue of all our titles, please write to
Christian Focus Publications,
Geanies House, Fearn,
Ross-shire, IV20 1TW, Great Britain

For details of our titles visit us on our web site
http://www.christianfocus.com

Other Christian Focus titles
by
Donald Macleod

A Faith to Live By
In this book the author examines the doctrines detailed in the Westminster Confession of Faith and applies them to the contemporary situation facing the church.

ISBN 1 85792 428 2   *Hardback*   *320 pages*

Behold Your God
A major work on the doctrine of God, covering his power, anger, righteousness, name and being. This book will educate and stimulate deeper thinking and worship.

ISBN 1 876 676 509   *paperback*   256 pages

Rome and Canterbury
This book assesses the attempts for unity between the Anglican and Roman Catholic churches, examining the argument of history, the place of Scripture, and the obstacle of the ordination of women.

ISBN 0 906 731 887   *paperback*   *64 pages*

The Spirit of Promise
This book gives advice on discovering our spiritual role in the local church, the Spirit's work in guidance, and discusses various interpretations of the baptism of the Spirit.

ISBN 0 906 731 448   *paperback*   *112 pages*

Shared Life
The author examines what the Bible teaches concerning the Trinity, then explores various historical and theological interpretations regarding the Trinity, before indicating where some of the modern cults err in their views of the Trinity.

ISBN 1-85792-128-3   *paperback*   *128 pages*